Finding and Restoring Longcase Clocks

Anthony Ells

The Crowood Press

First published in 2001 by
The Crowood Press Ltd
Ramsbury, Marlborough
Wiltshire SN8 2HR

Paperback edition 2009

British Library Cataloguing-in-Publication Data
A catalogue record for this book is available from the British Library.

ISBN 978 1 84797 135 7

Acknowledgements
I would like to express my gratitude to all those who assisted with this project,
including those who allowed me to photograph their clocks. In particular, I
would like to thank the following: Phillip Alexander for his efforts in restoring the
clock case, and for his helpful suggestions during the preparation of the text
describing his work; David Buxton MBHI for his skilled restoration to the dial,
and for supplying me with details of the procedures he used for inclusion in the
text covering dial restoration; Devon Clocks for allowing me to use an illustration
of their reproduction longcase clock movement; GK Hadfield for providing
photographs from their range of sale clocks for use in the colour section
(photographs taken by PWS Photography); Malcolm Wild FBHI for allowing me
to use the clock-hand silhouettes from his catalogue; Chris Baldwin MBHI and
my sister Susan for reading the manuscript and making helpful suggestions; my
sister Heather for her help with the computer and configuring the wordprocessor;
and Ivan Slee MBHI for providing details on the songwriter Henry Clay Work.

Disclaimer
The author and the publishers wish to point out that there are health and safety,
and environmental issues that must be addressed by all readers who involve
themselves in any form of clock making or restoration activity. Before using any
workshop tools, materials or chemicals of any description it is the reader's
responsibility to ensure that they are fully conversant with accepted and approved
procedures and practices for their safe use. This particularly applies to the
operation and use of any power or machine tools. All chemicals and some
consumable materials must be disposed of responsibly when their useful life is
over. Manufacturers' health and safety, and environmental recommendations
should be adhered to. If in the slightest doubt, always seek professional advice
before proceeding.

Typeface used: Plantin.

Typeset and designed by
D & N Publishing
Baydon, Marlborough, Wiltshire.

Printed and bound in Spain by Graphy Cems.

CONTENTS

1 EXAMPLES OF LONGCASE CLOCKS 5

2 CLOCK VALUES 15

3 PITFALLS TO AVOID WHEN PURCHASING A LONGCASE CLOCK........20

4 THE TIME TRAIN AND HOW IT WORKS 25

5 THE STRIKE TRAIN AND HOW IT WORKS 43

6 THE RESTORATION PROJECT 62

7 RESTORATION OF THE CLOCK CASE, DIAL AND HANDS....................74

8 RESTORATION OF THE CLOCK MOVEMENT 97

9 SETTING UP THE CLOCK 122

10 MAKING YOUR OWN CLOCK CASE.....................................132

FURTHER INFORMATION 138

GLOSSARY 141

INDEX 143

An assortment of longcase clocks and different dials.

1

EXAMPLES OF LONGCASE CLOCKS

There are many different types of clock, but a longcase clock (grandfather clock) is certainly the most majestic and perhaps the first image that most people would picture, if asked to think for a moment about clocks. Although all longcase clocks look similar at first glance, they were made in many different case styles and sizes. Some cases were made in one type of wood throughout, while others used a combination of more than one wood. A selection of typical longcase clocks is illustrated in the colour section for comparison.

BRIEF BACKGROUND TO LONGCASE CLOCKS

Early longcase clocks were incredibly expensive and the sole preserve of the fabulously wealthy. In those days (latter half of the seventeenth century), a longcase clock was regarded as a status symbol. They were generally placed in a position of prominence so as to impress visitors. Many years were to pass before longcase clocks reduced in price and, although still well made, the majority of later clocks lacked the exceptionally high build quality and refinement associated with early examples.

The fashion for this style of clock died out in the middle of the nineteenth century, but even then the cheapest example would have cost the equivalent of several years' wages for a working man. Fortunately, fashion has turned once more to favour the elegance and beauty of longcase clocks. These days, the later nineteenth century examples are within financial reach of most ordinary families.

CASES

Case Materials

The usual case materials to be found in antique clocks, in order of desirability, are as follows: walnut, mahogany, oak and pine. Often there is an inlay or marquetry work on hardwood cases that is usually in a contrasting wood. There are, however, examples to be found with ivory, mother-of-pearl, tortoiseshell or brass inlay. Antique clock cases in pine are almost always found stripped and waxed these days, but would have been painted when they were new.

Other types of wood were used to construct clock cases, but those listed above were the most common. Occasionally, ebonized or lacquered cases are found but these are very much an acquired taste, most buyers preferring a natural woodgrain finish. Carving on clock cases is another feature sometimes found, usually on oak cases, and it can look very attractive.

Clock cases made in oak are usually solid oak throughout with the possible exception of the backboard and hood top, which are often made from pine. Most of the cases made in more exotic woods are a veneered surface over a carcass, usually of oak, and again with a pine backboard. Case furniture such as escutcheons, capitals and finials are usually solid cast brass with a polished finish, although they are sometimes gilded. Locks and hinges can be made from brass but are often wrought iron, particularly in very old clocks.

Mass-produced reproduction longcase clocks, including grandmother and granddaughter clocks, made up until the 1950s were usually manufactured with solid wood mouldings and veneered plywood for the rest. Many of today's mass-produced offerings rarely contain any solid hardwood; instead, they are made from plywood or medium density fibreboard (MDF), sometimes given a veneer finish but mostly sprayed all over with a coloured lacquer specially formulated to give a simulated 'polished hardwood' look to the case.

Individual, high-quality handmade clock cases are still being made today in a choice of woods and styles and can be as finely crafted as a genuine antique. The advantage of having a new case made is being able to specify the size, style and type of wood used, and being certain that it will be in perfect condition when finished. The disadvantage is that the cost of having one of these cases made is very likely to exceed the total cost of a late antique clock.

Case Types

In Great Britain, longcase clocks were probably known as such from their beginnings in the seventeenth century. In the USA they are referred to as tallcase clocks, which is in fact a more apt description.

It is believed that the name 'grandfather clock', the popular terminology for a longcase clock, came into general use following the release of a song in 1876 entitled 'Grandfather's Clock', written by the American songwriter Henry Clay Work (1832–1884). Modern reproduction clocks are generally categorized as follows: grandfather clock, with an overall height of 6ft 6in (2.0m) or greater; grandmother clock, with an overall height of between 5ft 6in to 6ft 6in (1.7m to 2.0m); granddaughter clock, with an overall height of less than 5ft 6in (1.7m).

Many weight-driven reproduction longcase clocks have glazed trunk doors so that the brass weight shells and pendulum can be seen. Some early longcase clocks were fitted with a small round glass to the trunk door, known as a lenticular glass. These are about 4in (100mm) in diameter and usually positioned near the bottom of the door to correspond with the position of the pendulum bob. It is rarely possible to see the pendulum bob through a lenticular glass. The pendulum is right at the back of the case and the glass has

Grandfather's Clock

My Grandfather's clock was too tall for the shelf,
So it stood ninety years on the floor;
It was taller by half than the old man himself,
Though it weighed not a pennyweight more.
It was bought on the morn of the day that he was
   born,
It was always his treasure and his pride;
But it stopped short – never to go again –
When the old man died.

Chorus
Ninety years without slumbering (tick, tick, tick,
   tick),
His life seconds numbering (tick, tick, tick, tick),
It stopped short – never to go again –
When the old man died.

In watching its pendulum swing to and fro,
Many hours had he spent while a boy;
And its childhood and manhood the clock seemed
   to know
And to share both his grief and his joy.
For it struck twenty-four when he entered at the door,
With a blooming and beautiful bride;
But it stopped short – never to go again –
When the old man died.

Chorus

My grandfather said that of those he could hire,
Not a servant so faithful he found;
For it wasted no time, and had but one desire –
At the close of each week to be wound.
And it kept in its place – not a frown on its face,
And the hands never hung by its side;
But it stopped short – never to go again –
When the old man died.

Chorus

It rang an alarm in the dead of the night –
An alarm that for years had been dumb;
And we knew that his spirit was pluming for flight –
That his hour of departure had come.
Still the clock kept the time, with a soft and
   muffled chime,
As we silently stood by his side;
But it stopped short – never to go again –
When the old man died.

Chorus

Words and music by Henry Clay Work, written in 1876 and dedicated to his sister Lizzie.

insufficient area to enable enough light to penetrate in order to see the pendulum swinging.

Another type of clock in a tallcase, often mistaken for a longcase clock, is the regulator. Regulators are superior in every way to the ordinary longcase clock and are highly prized by collectors. They have high-quality cases, usually of plain classical design, and a very distinctive dial layout. Unlike ordinary longcase clocks, regulators usually have a glazed trunk door. This is to show off the quality and workmanship of the special temperature-compensated pendulums which are a feature of regulator clocks.

Another feature of regulators, easily seen through the trunk door, would be the large brass weight pulley and single weight with polished brass shell. The pulley is often two or three times the diameter of an ordinary longcase pulley wheel and is finely crossed out. The stirrup is also of brass as a rule and beautifully styled with a hook for hanging the weight. On some clocks, the wheel and stirrup assembly are engraved.

DIAL TYPES

Dials are another clock feature with many variations, particularly in shape, size and the materials used in their manufacture. Whatever the height of a clock and irrespective of whether it is an antique or a modern reproduction, the shape, size and type of dial are among the main criteria referred to when describing a clock. The most common are square dials and break-arch dials (a square dial with a half-moon shape on the top). Of the two types, break-arch dials date from a later period than square dials.

Some clocks have round dials and if the hood is also round in shape, narrowing to a neck somewhere below the four and eight o'clock position when viewed from the front, they are often referred to as Drum Head clocks. Very occasionally, a clock may be seen with an oval dial although these are very rare. Each dial type can be found in a range of sizes and it is usual to refer to the size in inches. The size is measured across the width of the dial from one side to the other

and parallel to the bottom edge, or the diameter for round dials.

Square dials are usually either brass with silvered chapter ring (the ring bearing the numerals one to twelve in Arabic or Roman style) or steel with a painted surface. Round dials, including regulator dials, are usually painted, although some have a silvered surface. Oval dials are usually painted. Early break-arch dials are brass with silvered chapter rings; later examples are usually painted, although some were entirely silvered. Painted dials are also referred to as White Dials.

Some break-arch dials are found where the arch is a separate piece attached to a square dial. These may have been modifications carried out by the original maker, who perhaps received an order for a clock with a break-arch dial and decided to modify a square dial he held in stock. Alternatively, the customer may have asked for his square dial clock to be modified to look like the newer break-arch design.

Brass break-arch dial with an old father time rocking feature and an unusual silvered dial centre.

The arched portion of a dial may display any one of a number of features. If it is a painted dial there is usually a painted scene in this area. A brass or silvered dial would have either a cartouche with arch spandrels or engraving. Sometimes there may be a lever shaped something like a clock hand in the centre of the arch which, when given half a turn, disables the clock's striking mechanism.

Another popular feature found in some break-arch dials is moon phase indication, in which a section of the arch is cut out to reveal a picture of the moon painted on a disc of thin metal. The disc is free to revolve behind the dial cut-out and is turned a small amount each day by the working clock movement.

When looking at the clock each day, the painting of the moon is seen to appear gradually, from the left of the cut-out, until eventually a full moon becomes visible. The disc continues turning a little each day to show the moon gradually waning until it disappears to the right of the cut-out. In fact, the disc has two paintings of the moon on it, so that when the old moon goes out of sight, the other painting is in position to appear as the new moon.

Some clocks have rocking features or an automaton in the break-arch. There are many different themes, but often a sailing ship is shown slowly rocking on the water. A coastal scene is painted in the arch with the area of the sea and part of the sky cut out and removed from the dial. The sea and sky are painted onto a separate back-plate somewhat larger in area than the cut-out in the dial and spaced a little way behind it. When the painted scene is viewed from the front of the clock, it is not obvious that a cut-out exists.

The profile of a ship is produced in thin metal and painted to show all the features usually associated with a sailing ship, such as sails and rigging, and in scale with the painted scene on the dial. The bottom of the ship is attached to the top of a thin rod, the other end of which is clamped to the pallet arbor in the clock movement.

The ship is held in the narrow gap between the cut-out in the arch, and the painted plate showing the sea and sky is positioned behind it. Because the ship is attached to the pallet arbor via the thin rod, this effectively makes the ship an extension of the pendulum rod. Therefore, as the pendulum swings, the ship will rock very slightly side to side as though riding the waves. Other examples can be found where the rocking feature is pivoted through the dial and driven from behind.

Most regulator clocks have a particular style of dial layout known as a regulator dial. The dials are usually round and have only the minutes marked around the outside and numbered at five-minute intervals. There are two small subsidiary dials; one of these is set above the main dial centre and indicates seconds, while the other one is set below the main dial centre and indicates the hours. There is just one hand coming from the centre of the dial and this indicates the minutes. Each of the two subsidiary dials has a single hand of its own. Reading a regulator dial can be confusing to anyone not familiar with the layout – the minutes are read off in the usual way from the big hand, but the hour is read off the small lower subsidiary dial.

Spandrels

Spandrel is the name given to the triangular-shaped area at the corners on clock dials. Brass dials usually have cast-brass spandrels with either a polished or gilded finish. Silvered dials have engraved spandrels, if they have any at all. Painted dials invariably have painted spandrels (floral decoration or shells are popular, although some have painted pastoral scenes).

On a brass break-arch dial, if there is no moon phase indication or rocking feature, there will usually be a round central embellishment of some kind with arch spandrels either side. Silvered break-arch dials might have engraved arch spandrels either side of a round central feature. Different spandrel styles provide a valuable guide to dating antique clocks.

Hands

Early clock hands were cut from sheet steel or brass, entirely by hand. They range in style from the classically plain to the incredibly ornate. A pair of fancy longcase clock hands, in steel, could take a skilled man with a piercing saw many hours to make. Brass, being a softer material,

Silhouettes of assorted clock hands, cut out by hand.

would be a little quicker to cut. After a pair of hands had been cut out, they would have had to be filed to thin down the outside edges and taper the thickness of the hand from the boss to the tip. The boss of each hand would then have to be made to fit the clock movement. The final operation would be to polish the front surface of each hand in preparation for bluing.

Modern mass-produced clock hands are not manufactured in the same way. They are stamped or etched out of much thinner material and left parallel in thickness, with no skilled hand-fettling to improve their appearance. They lack the quality and character of the handcrafted item – the surface finish, instead of being a beautiful heat-induced blue oxide, is usually black paint.

CLOCK MOVEMENTS

The standard layout for a striking clock movement comprises two separate sets of gear wheels known as wheel trains. One wheel train drives the hands and is known as the going or time train. The other drives the hammer, to strike the hours on a bell or gong, and is known as the strike train. A clock with no striking work at all it is referred to as a timepiece.

Another feature referred to when describing a clock is the running time of the clock for one winding: thirty-hour, eight-day, fifteen-day, month-going or more. Clocks that were made to run for one month or more at a single winding are comparatively rare, and are consequently very sought-after by collectors. The majority of longcase clocks are fitted with either eight-day or thirty-hour movements.

With seven days in one week and twenty-four hours in one day, why have eight-day and thirty-hour movements? The answer is in order to provide a factor of safety. If a clock is not wound when it has run down, it is obvious the clock will stop. Take as an example a clock that will run for eight days. It is always best to wind any clock at the same time, on the same day of each week. If the owner, for some reason, is unable to wind the clock at the usual time there is up to one day's grace before the clock becomes completely run down and stops.

Some antique longcase clocks were made with chiming movements. These should not to be confused with the modern mass-produced chiming movements. The antique version is very much more robust than its modern imitator, and was made and finished to a much higher standard.

A lot of the early twentieth-century mass-produced British and German movements were quite nicely made with reasonably thick plates. The modern versions are nearly all German, and with stiff competition between manufacturers, costs have been trimmed wherever possible. One of the first casualties of cost-cutting is clock plate thickness. Brass is relatively expensive and reducing plate thickness, by even a small amount, will reduce costs. However, it is generally accepted that the thinner a clock plate has been made, the sooner the pivot holes will wear and need bushing to restore them to their original condition.

Eight-Day Clocks
The typical eight-day longcase clock has two wheel trains. Each wheel train is mounted side by side between a front and backplate, and each is driven by a separate weight acting on a wire or gut line wrapped around its driving barrel. The clock is wound once a week by means of a cranked key used on each of the square winding arbors, visible through winding holes in the dial. These movements are referred to as plate or plated movements.

Usually, eight-day clocks can be recognized from a distance by the presence of winding holes in the dial. This, however, is not a foolproof method, as some makers used eight-day dials on their thirty-hour clocks and fitted dummy winding squares behind the winding holes to make them look like a more expensive eight-day clock.

Thirty-Hour Clocks
There are two types of thirty-hour movement. The later type looks very similar to an eight-day movement, with two wheel trains side by side between a front and backplate. An earlier design has the two wheel trains arranged in tandem with the going train at the front of the movement and the strike train behind it. In this design the

plates, which are more or less square in shape, are arranged one at the top and one at the bottom. There is a pillar at each corner, between the plates, holding them together in the form of a one-piece cage. There are three fairly narrow strips of brass forming the bearing or pivot plates for the wheel trains. These are fitted in line between the top and bottom plates, one at the front, one in the middle and one at the back. The pivot plates are removable to allow assembly of the wheel trains. This type of movement is referred to as a birdcage or posted movement.

Looking at the movement from the side, the front pivot plate, fitted just inside the front edge of the cage, is provided with the pivot holes for the front of the going train. The pivot plate that is fitted to the middle of the movement is provided with pivot holes for both the rear of the

going train and the front of the strike train. The back pivot plate is provided with pivot holes for the rear of the strike train.

The big difference between eight-day and thirty-hour movements, apart from the running duration for one winding, is the method of driving the clock. The eight-day movement has two weights, one for each train. The thirty-hour movement has only one weight and it drives both trains via an ingenious system using an endless rope. There are two driving pulleys, one of which drives the going train and the other the striking train. Each of the driving pulleys is fitted with a number of spikes standing up from the bottom of the rope grooves to engage the rope and prevent it from slipping.

The rope is threaded through the clock and over the drive pulleys before the ends are spliced

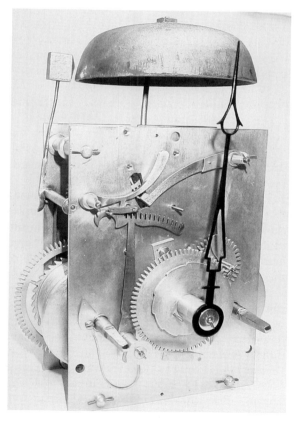

Typical eight-day movement, front view.

Thirty-hour movement, front view. This movement has a dummy winding square fitted to the lower right side of the front plate. The dummy left-hand square is attached to the back of the dial.

Thirty-hour posted or birdcage movement.

Layout of chain and weights for a thirty-hour clock.

or sewn together, forming an endless loop of rope. There are two other items threaded onto the rope before the ends are joined. The loop of rope on the idle side of the drive pulleys is threaded through a ring-shaped lead weight called a doughnut. The idea of the doughnut weight is to keep the rope slightly taught on the idle side of the two drive pulleys, thus preventing it from riding up and coming out of the grooves.

The loop of rope on the other side of the drive pulleys is threaded through a small idler pulley, on to which the heavy driving weight is hooked. By arranging things in this way, one weight will drive both wheel trains quite independently. The strike train driving pulley is provided with a ratchet mechanism between it and the strike drive wheel, enabling the pulley to be turned backwards when the idle side of the rope is pulled

each day, raising the drive weight and thus winding the clock.

Today, most thirty-hour clocks have been converted from rope to chain drive, thus eliminating the need for frequent rope changes caused by the spikes in the drive pulleys damaging the rope. This conversion necessitates changing both of the rope pulleys for pulleys that will operate with a chain. Pulley conversion kits and the chain for thirty-hour clocks are still available today from clock material dealers. The problem with chain-converted clocks is that the replacement chain pulleys are very crude. They are little more than flat-bottomed rope pulleys with slightly shorter and less pointed spikes standing out from the bottom of the grooves.

Even when new, this system is inefficient, but after a period of running it becomes very rough

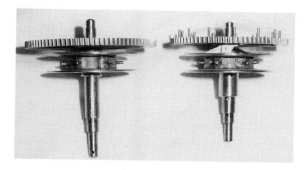

Thirty-hour chain pulleys.

in its transmission of power. The roughness is mainly due to each individual chain link wearing and stretching a little in use, causing the centre distance of each link to become a little further apart. Then, instead of the chain links falling nicely onto each spike of the drive wheel pulley, every so often a link will catch on a spike tip. The chain is then lifted up and out of its groove as the wheel turns, only to slip down in again when the wheel turns a little further, causing the chain to snatch. The only way to cure this is to use pulleys with teeth shaped like the modern German chain-driven movements.

CHIMING MOVEMENTS

Chiming movements, sometimes called three-train or quarter-chiming movements, have in addition to the usual time and strike train a third train that drives musical chimes. The chimes sound every quarter hour and, after the hour chime has sounded, the strike train is released to strike the hour.

There are a number of different chimes, the most common being the Westminster, Whittington and St Michael. Some clocks have all three chimes available. By simply moving a lever on the dial it is possible to select whichever chime is required at the time. The chimes usually sound on a nest of eight bells situated in line, at the top of the movement. Some late clocks, instead of having bells, were fitted with sets of long tubular gongs, suspended inside the back of the case.

REPRODUCTION MOVEMENTS

Most reproduction clocks from grandfather to granddaughter use chiming movements. The chime and strike for these clocks is usually produced on a tuned set of steel or bronze gong rods fitted inside the hood. These movements can be either spring-wound or weight-driven. If weight-driven, it is usually with chains, although some manufacturers use wire lines. The chain-drive system used on this type of movement is totally different from the previously mentioned antique thirty-hour clocks. In this case, the chain wheel is of a much more modern design, with teeth shaped more like the teeth on a bicycle chain sprocket as opposed to the pins fitted to antique clocks.

Just like the teeth on a bicycle sprocket, the modern clock wheel teeth have a chamfer around each tooth tip to help the chain link to fit over nicely as the wheel turns. This prevents the chain from catching on the tooth tips and 'riding up' out of the groove. These movements will run very smoothly without any of the annoying jerks or snatching associated with antique chain-driven clocks.

Modern chain sprocket (pulley).

Almost without exception, all reproduction longcase clocks run for eight days per winding. Modern movements have an extra wheel and pinion in the wheel train compared to antique movements. This is referred to as the intermediate wheel and pinion and it is fitted between the main driving wheel, or great wheel, and the centre wheel. The use of an intermediate wheel greatly reduces the number of turns of the great wheel in each twenty-four-hour period. As a result of this a single length of line or chain can be used, the weight only needing a clear drop of approximately 3ft to give one week of running time.

Although mass-produced movements are not made and finished to the same high standard as antique movements, they will give a perfectly satisfactory performance and last for many years if properly restored.

Intermediate wheel.

DRIVING WEIGHTS

Driving weights vary in size from one clock to another, but generally they weigh anything from 8–14lb (3.6–6.4kg) each for the average antique clock. It is not uncommon to find that one weight is larger and heavier than the other. If the weights are different, the heaviest one usually goes on the strike side as there is more load on the striking wheel train. Nobody in fact knows whether the clocks were made with odd-sized weights from new. It is possible that over the years weights became muddled up at a clockmaker's workshop, or, in some cases, a weight may have been deliberately changed for a heavier one in order to make the clock work instead of having it serviced.

Each weight should be just heavy enough to make its respective wheel train run satisfactorily with the movement in good order. If the strike runs rapidly, with no fault in the movement to account for this, then the weight should be changed for a lighter one. If the pendulum swing is excessive and the bob comes very close to the case sides, it would be advisable to try a lighter weight.

Antique weights are usually made from cast iron or lead, with a wrought iron or steel hook cast in place at the top of the weight. The finish given to these parts is nothing special as they are not visible unless the waist door is open. Regulator clocks and almost all reproduction clocks, where the trunk door is glazed, have weights with an outer shell of brass, the surface finish being either grained or polished and then lacquered.

Modern weights have the inside filled with either lead shot, lead rings or steel rings. These are factory adjusted until the correct driving weight is achieved. Antique brass weights, on the other hand, usually had molten lead poured into the brass shell to fill them and they were not intended to be adjustable. It is worth mentioning that antique three-train movements usually have much larger weights than standard longcase movements. The chime-driving weights on some of these clocks can be truly massive.

2 CLOCK VALUES

The value of antique clocks depends on a number of factors, the main considerations being age, maker, style and material of case and any complicated technical features of the movement. A nicely proportioned antique longcase clock made in mahogany or walnut with a good colour and grain figuring will always be worth more money than a plain oak case of similar style and age. A similar clock dating from an earlier period, or with a highly regarded maker's name on the dial or movement, would add significantly to the clock's value.

Mechanical complications, including those which also enhance the appearance of the dial, such as moon phase indication or rocking features in the break-arch, will further enhance the value of a given clock. Any unusual mechanical functions performed by the clock, such as perpetual calendar or tide indication, would again add to its value. Mass-produced reproduction clocks also come in a wide range of sizes, case styles, finishes and build quality, but values would always be a lot less than for an antique clock or even a quality handmade reproduction clock.

Eight-day clocks are more sought after than thirty-hour clocks because most people would prefer to wind their clock only once a week. The value of a thirty-hour clock, therefore, will usually be quite a lot less than that of an eight-day clock of comparable quality, age and style. In reality, opening the waist door of a longcase clock and pulling the rope or chain to wind it takes only two minutes at the most. If done as you walk past the clock either first thing in the morning or last thing at night, it soon becomes an instinctive act and presents no inconvenience.

It is unlikely that any clock of great horological importance would be offered for sale other than through one of the big auction houses, probably a London firm or a specialist clock dealer. It is even less likely that one would be sold at a knock-down price. There are, however, many opportunities for those looking to buy a more modest clock at a realistic price.

AUCTION GUIDE PRICES

It is only possible to indicate clock values as an approximate guide in any book of this type. There are many variable factors to take into consideration. Ever-changing world economics, supply and demand and the influence of fashion affect the value of many things, including antiques, collectables and new luxury items, clocks being no exception. Also, for the reasons discussed previously, practically every clock you see will, to some extent, have a different specification, age or condition and these differences will affect values.

You should, however, expect to pay very similar prices for unrestored clocks, whether buying at auction or from antique fairs and clock fairs. Take, as an example, longcase clocks of the 1850s. Let us assume plain oak cases, painted dials, reasonably tidy original condition, complete and in working order, but not restored. At auction, you could expect thirty-hour clocks to sell for around £400–£1,000 and eight-day clocks for £1,200–£2,500. If the clock is in poor condition or made up with parts taken from another clock, it may well sell for less. If the clock is of earlier date or in above-average condition, the price is likely to be greater.

Mass-produced grandmother and grand-daughter clocks from the 1930s usually have solid oak mouldings and oak veneer plywood panels and come with either round, square or break-arch dials. Cases range from plain 4ft 6in high arched top to 6ft 6in high break-arch with swan neck pediment. Most come with Westminster chiming movements, the smaller clocks being spring-driven, the larger ones usually weight-driven. Auction prices for tidy examples, complete but not necessarily working, range from around £75 to £500.

Modern-day equivalents of the 1930s clocks, where the cases are made of chipboard or MDF and the panels are held together with plastic fixings similar to kitchen unit fixings, are not worth bothering with. The quality of just about every aspect of these clocks is so poor that, no matter how much time and money is spent on them, they are likely to be a disappointment.

When buying from auctions and fairs you have to take your chances with what is offered. Even if the clocks prove to be in working order, it is rare to find that they have been professionally restored. Most auctioneers' conditions of sale contain a clause barring any comeback if it later transpires that you have bought a 'pig in a poke'. Reputable clock dealers, on the other hand, will offer a minimum of twelve months' guarantee with clocks they sell. Any restoration work will usually have been carried out to a high standard, ensuring that the clock is in good working order. It must also be borne in mind that a dealer's price will usually include VAT, delivering the clock to your home and setting it up properly. Because dealers offer this level of service and have the added expense of maintaining retail premises, their prices are bound to be higher than those at auction.

Before setting out to buy a clock it would be advisable to visit as many auction houses as possible and observe clocks being sold. Compare the age, condition and specifications of various clocks and try to ascertain their approximate values. Treat any auctioneers' guide prices with caution, as these are usually deliberately set low to encourage people to attend in the mistaken belief that they will pick up a cheap clock. Study reference material, including published lists giving up-to-date prices achieved at auction. A popular reference source is *Miller's Clocks and Barometers Buyer's Guide*, but beware, some of the prices quoted are a long way off the norm. Attend local antique and clock fairs and compare prices with those achieved at auction.

In addition, visit as many clock dealers' showrooms as you can. Study closely all the different features, styles and specifications, not forgetting age, and note how these affect the asking price. Practise until you are confident enough to be able to judge fairly accurately the retail price of any clock you may see in a showroom before looking at its price tag. Compare showroom retail prices with auction prices, taking into account any restoration costs.

If you intend finding a clock in a distressed state and restoring it yourself, or have someone restore it for you, it would be advantageous to carry out this valuation exercise first. Only by knowing what a clock in restored condition is likely to be worth will you be able to decide how much to pay for it in a neglected condition. One very important point to bear in mind when comparing prices is that the older an antique clock is, the more valuable it will be for the same specification.

WHERE TO FIND A CLOCK

There are several possibilities to consider when looking to buy a clock. You may decide to take the easy and quickest route and buy from a reputable clock dealer. You could look around the various showrooms until you find a clock you like. It would almost certainly be fully restored, guaranteed and the price would usually include delivery to and setting up in your home. If you do decide to take this route, you should be prepared to pay the top price for the clock.

Classified advertisements in local papers and weekly 'for sale' publications occasionally prove worthwhile. Some general antique shops sell clocks and they are worth a look. Auctions are always worth checking as clocks are often sold this way. Antique fairs and particularly clockfairs are a very good source. Internet 'sealed bid' auctions and web sites advertising antique clocks for sale are a very recent development you may wish to consider.

Buying from Classified Advertisements

There are two main points to consider before buying from classified advertisements. First of all, just as with any other business, there are a few unscrupulous traders around and some will try to sell a clock privately through the small ads without declaring that they are 'trade'. By doing this they hope to avoid any comeback if you later discover that the clock is not as it was described to be. Traders, unlike bona fide clock dealers, are not necessarily knowledgeable horologists with a good reputation to maintain.

The second point to consider is travelling distance to view the clock. Even if the advertiser is a genuine member of the public selling the clock privately, it is not unknown for people to exaggerate when describing their clock over the telephone. This is not so bad if you have only travelled a short distance, but to find that you have been deliberately misled after driving fifty miles or more can be annoying. Despite these drawbacks, there are bargains to be had from the classified columns and this source need not be dismissed altogether.

If you find a clock you like and a price is agreed, do establish with the vendor that the clock is theirs to sell before parting with any money. Always make sure you get a signed receipt, which ideally should include a good description of the clock, clearly stating any identifying marks, particularly names.

Buying from General Antique Shops

It is quite the norm these days to find at least one antique shop in towns throughout the UK. They range from the smart high street antique shop to the downmarket back street bric-a-brac shop. The smart establishments usually sell high-quality restored goods for which they expect top prices. The smaller back street bric-a-brac shops occasionally have clocks for sale, but although these may be working they are unlikely to have been properly restored. There is often a reluctance by these establishments to offer much of a guarantee, which could be viewed as a lack of confidence in the reliability of the clock they are selling.

Buying from Auctions

If you look up 'auction rooms' and 'auctioneers and valuers' in your local directory, you will probably find a number of listings. Some of the bigger firms have specialist sales for clocks three or four times a year. Many of them will hold regular general sales and house-clearance sales, usually twice a month, and these will often include cheaper clocks.

Unless otherwise stated in the catalogue, or by the auctioneer at the time of the sale, each lot is sold as seen with all descriptions given in good faith. It is the sole responsibility of the bidders to satisfy themselves that all is well before bidding. Most auction houses offer viewing for at least one day before the actual day of the auction. If there is some aspect of the clock you are uncertain about, this will give you a little time to check it out before the sale starts.

It is very likely that if you are unknown to the auctioneers, and you want to pay by cheque, they will insist on clearing your cheque before allowing you to take the clock. The best way around this is to discuss the matter with the auctioneers before the day of the sale and, if they still insist on clearing your cheque first, you might consider taking cash with you, up to the limit you are prepared to pay for the clock.

It is worth remembering that most auction houses require prospective bidders to register with them before the auction starts. Once you have registered, you are usually given a card or a paddle with your bid number printed on it. You use this to make your bid for any of the lots that interest you. On the fall of the hammer, the successful bidder holds their card or paddle aloft so that the auctioneer can read the number.

If you intend bidding, the first priority is to write down the numbers of the lots you are interested in, or mark them in the catalogue if there is one. You should then decide the maximum amount you are prepared to pay for each particular lot. The auctioneer will call out the lot numbers before each one is auctioned. When the lot four or five numbers before the one you are interested in is called, manoeuvre yourself into a position where the auctioneer will be able to see you easily. If the bidding is brisk and rapidly approaching your personal price limit, wait and see what happens. If the bidding is slow, providing it is below your limit, make a clear bid so that your interest in the lot is registered with the auctioneer and take it from there. Once your limit has been reached, stop bidding and walk away before you are tempted to pay more than you had intended.

Buying from Antique and Clock Fairs

There are exceptions to every rule, but generally if you arrive at an antique fair after 8.00am you can expect the real bargains to be long gone. Specialist clock fairs are different, in that they usually have a published time when the general public will be admitted. However, if you are prepared to pay a premium, you could be admitted up to one hour before the general public under the guise of a 'trade pass'. This seems to be nothing more than a way for the organizers of the event to make more money, as no proof of business activity is required. It seems they rely on a few individuals being prepared to pay a premium for the opportunity to have the first crack at any bargains before the gates are opened officially.

Some traders run their business full time, whereas for others it is a hobby; either way, most of them will only be interested in cash payments for their goods. This is quite understandable as they may have travelled a great distance to the venue and are unlikely to know anyone there. With no way of checking a prospective customer's credentials, most feel cash is their safest option. Cash is also a powerful bargaining tool and if you are prepared to haggle on price most traders would accept a reasonable offer.

Buying On-Line

The Internet is rapidly changing the way we search for and buy most things, including antiques. It is a fairly safe bet that whatever you are looking for someone, somewhere in the world, has one for sale. Searching on the Internet, particularly for something very unusual, is the easiest and most convenient way to find it.

If you do use this medium and you find a clock that appeals to you, ask for a comprehensive and detailed description. Photographs taken from different viewpoints will be useful. All this material including photographs can be sent as a file attachment via e-mail. If after studying the information you are still interested in the clock and you feel the asking price is reasonable, arrange a visit to view if this is possible. It would be unwise to buy an antique clock on the Internet 'sight unseen' unless you know and trust the vendor.

BUYING HINTS

Only buy a clock if you really like it. Ultimately, you will find it easier to live with a clock you love, even if you did pay a little over the odds for it, than one you dislike but bought on the cheap. When examining the clock of your choice be thorough and ask questions regarding any repair or restoration work that may have been carried out. Ask about the history and age of the clock and whether or not it is original.

One very important consideration is transport. Unless you buy from a clock dealer, you will have to get the clock home yourself. Not every one has a vehicle suitable for moving a longcase clock. If your own vehicle is too small and you do not happen to have a friend who owns a large estate car or van, you may have to hire a suitable vehicle, the cost of which should be taken into account when budgeting for your clock.

If you buy from an antique or clock fair, bear in mind that some of the traders travel long distances to attend these events and arrive in the early hours of the morning. With a one-day fair these traders often start packing up by mid-afternoon ready to get away before the rush. Should they have a clock you wish to purchase, this could leave you with insufficient time to make transport arrangements before they leave. If all else fails, you may be able to persuade the trader to deliver the clock to your home for an agreed extra payment.

When you are ready to make your purchase, you could telephone all the auction houses within a reasonable travelling distance and apply to go on their mailing list. They usually ask for a modest payment to cover the cost of their catalogues and the postage for a period of six or twelve months. The catalogues usually arrive a week or so before the auction date, giving you the chance to study the contents from the comfort of your armchair.

3 PITFALLS TO AVOID WHEN PURCHASING A LONGCASE CLOCK

DIAL AND MOVEMENT MARRIAGES

Original integrity is very important for antique clocks. If the dial has been changed or the movement and dial are not the ones originally fitted to the case, or many of the original parts have been replaced at some time, this will reduce the value of a clock. Dial and movement marriages, as they are called, are quite common and even to the trained eye they can be difficult to spot.

Close scrutiny of the dial back and movement front plate will usually reveal evidence of any marriage. Look for redundant holes in both the dial back and movement front plate where dial feet may have been fitted previously. Dial feet are the brass posts riveted to the back of the dial, the outer ends of which fit into mating holes in the movement front plate where they are pinned in place. The purpose of dial feet is to hold the dial firmly in place and space it away from the front

Dial back, showing new false plate made to fit the movement. Note the professionally added break arch, probably by the original maker.

Front view of the same dial showing dial centre fitted to the new false plate; the chapter ring will cover the black area.

plate of the movement so as to clear the motion work and other parts.

Very often, a false plate is fitted between the dial and movement front plate. False plates are often made from cast iron and are very brittle. They can be fitted with either three or four feet for attaching to the movement front plate and three or four holes to accept the dial feet. Look for evidence of dial feet holes being elongated, or redrilled to accept a non-original dial where the false plate belongs to the movement. Alternatively, if the false plate belongs to the dial, look for signs of the feet having been moved on the false plate or new holes in the movement front plate.

If the dial frame in the hood does not closely fit the dial, or does not have a small, even overlap, all the way round the dial edge, there is a good chance that something is not original. A dial which is obviously too large or too small to fit the dial frame in the hood is much easier to spot and the clock should be carefully scrutinized.

CASE REBUILDS

Extensive case rebuilds are another thing to look out for, as they also devalue a clock. Often, small areas of a clock case are found to be damaged and in need of repair. If any mouldings or case decorations are missing these would have to be made. So long as any new parts are made in the style of the original, preferably in wood of the same age as the rest of the case, all should be well. If, however, parts of the case are made from new wood it reduces the antique authenticity of the whole case. Should large areas be repaired with new wood, the clock can no longer realistically be claimed to be antique.

If you are buying an inexpensive, late nineteenth-century country clock, the above points are not quite so serious, providing the price is not too outrageous for its general condition and type. If, on the other hand, you are spending a lot of money for an early example, sold as genuine and all original but later found to be extensively rebuilt, this would be altogether more serious.

INCOMPLETE CLOCKS

Sometimes, incomplete clocks can be found for sale, usually a complete case but with no movement – although occasionally the basic movement is there, but with the dial or some of the parts missing. There are a few firms specializing in the supply of old clock movements and movements complete with dials; they also supply antique parts separately such as dials, pendulums, weights and pulleys and so on. It is surprising just how much money an incomplete clock, in a distressed condition, will make. This

The complete dial fitted to the movement. Note how the hand and barrel arbors protrude too far through the dial.

may be because someone either needs a case for a movement and dial they already possess, or vice versa.

Some clocks are even deliberately broken up when more money can be made by selling the movement and dial complete with pendulum and weights as one lot and the complete case as another lot. For the inexperienced, it is probably better to avoid incomplete clocks as there is a very real danger that the sum of all the parts will exceed the value of the finished clock.

BILL OF SALE

Wherever you buy your clock, if the vendor is reluctant to give you a proper receipt, think twice before you part with your money. No honest citizen or dealer would have any reason not to give a proper receipt for any money paid to them. If you come across this problem there could be an ominous reason for it, perhaps the clock has been stolen or, for other reasons, is not theirs to sell.

BAD RESTORATION WORK

Bad restoration work is a serious problem to be wary of. Amateurish attempts at dial or case restoration are the easiest to spot, but can be the hardest to rectify. Bad workmanship can seriously devalue a clock. The patina on wooden clock cases and the crazing of painted dial backgrounds are the result of many years, centuries in some cases, of natural maturing. If these surfaces are treated unsympathetically they may be damaged permanently and the clock would be spoilt.

If a painted dial is so badly damaged or rusted that the ground needs repainting, there are special procedures employed by professional dial restorers who undertake this type of work. The aim is to lessen the impact of a newly painted surface and to replicate, as accurately as possible, the original painted decoration and lettering in the appropriate style. If the work is done well, it is the next best thing to a sound original dial, although to the trained eye it would be easy to spot.

Dial back with added break arch; not as originally manufactured.

Front view of the same dial. Note the name, John Fisher Preston, on the break arch, and Holinel Liverpool, on the dial centre.

The clock with the hood fitted; note how the name on the break arch is masked by the top of the hood door frame.

Check the movement for obvious signs of damage, botched repairs or missing parts. Unless the movement has been professionally restored recently, there is likely to be evidence of wear. This is not unusual but must be taken into consideration when estimating the cost of restoring the clock. If the clock works, even if only for a few minutes, there is a good chance that nothing is missing.

PROBLEMS WITH BUYING AT AUCTION

When buying at auction do not allow the auctioneer to coax a further bid out of you if the price has reached the limit of your valuation or budget. This is a ploy often used by auctioneers if bidding stops short of the reserve price. Some people, in the heat of the moment, will carry on bidding after their price has been reached to prevent being 'out done' by their opponent. To do this is a serious error you would be well advised to avoid.

Auction prices can vary considerably. The main reason for this is that, at the very least, two seriously interested buyers are required to bid against one another, in order to achieve a high hammer price. Any clock attracting such attention and selling for a high price could be entered in the same auction room, in the same condition, some weeks later and sell for a lot less the second time if there was only one person present who was seriously interested in buying it. The reverse is also true, which is why it is important to know the value of clocks.

If buying at auction, always check for the dreaded 'buyer's premium'. If there is one, it is usually set at a minimum of 10 per cent of the hammer price and is paid by the purchaser in addition to the hammer price. This fee is also subject to VAT at the ruling rate and will come as a nasty surprise if you are unaware of it.

Another very important point to check is whether or not the clock itself is being sold subject to VAT. If it is entered for sale by a VAT-registered company and forms part of their assets, the entire hammer price will be liable for VAT. If in doubt, check with the auctioneers before the auction starts. For the record, antique dealers and antique clock specialists usually operate a Customs and Excise approved retail scheme whereby VAT is only calculated on the profit element and not the full retail price.

CLASSIFIED ADVERTISEMENTS

When looking at classified advertisements, you will sometimes find the asking price for a clock is unrealistically high. Some people put a value on their clock based on similar clocks they have seen in a dealer's showroom, but fail to take into account condition, restoration costs and all the benefits of buying from a dealer, particularly the guarantee.

4 THE TIME TRAIN AND HOW IT WORKS

The following information will give a basic understanding of what goes on behind the dial of a conventional longcase clock. It is not a highly detailed thesis covering all the variations found in clock movements. The intention is to explain, in simple terms, the fundamental principle involved.

The general appearance, size and layout of most movements, of the same running duration, are very similar for all antique longcase clocks. Almost without exception they are all well designed and made, but some are made and finished to a superior standard. There are different methods for effecting date and moon phase changes, ranging from the very basic to the elaborate. A few clocks have complicated and technically advanced features, while the design and arrangement of strike mechanisms and escapements between different makers is a fascinating study.

Fancy shaped profiles given to clock plates and pillars, or hand-engraved decorations to plates and associated parts are purely aesthetic enhancements. It is, however, the style of these enhancements that can often provide the key when attempting to date clocks. This can be especially helpful if the maker's name cannot be found on the clock, or the name is not documented in any of the standard reference books.

Twentieth-century mass-produced movements are also found with varied designs between manufacturers. Some of the design features, common to mass-produced movements, are not usually found on antique clock movements and vice versa.

However, despite all the design variations and the differences between eight-day and thirty-hour and antique or reproduction movements, the working principles are the same. The easiest way to understand how a clock works is to take, as an example, a simple timepiece and study each of the five main subsections of the clock movement in turn. Once the basic principles are understood they may be applied to any movement studied in the future, whether antique or reproduction.

THE FIVE CLOCK MOVEMENT SUBSECTIONS

Clock movements may be divided up into five subsections as follows.

- First, there is a power source. This can be a weight, electricity (mains or battery) or a mainspring, and it is used to drive the clock. All traditional antique longcase clocks, and many of the larger reproduction versions, are weight-driven.
- Second, there is a wheel train. This is the name given to the gear wheels that transmit the drive from the power source to the escapement of the clock.
- Third, there is the escapement, which is a device that prevents the gear train from running unhindered, but lets it go (escape) a very small measured amount at each beat of the oscillator.
- Fourth, is the oscillator, usually either a balance or pendulum, which is responsible for maintaining the precise intervals of time between each of the escaping actions of the escapement. In a longcase clock the oscillator takes the form of a pendulum.
- Last, there is the motion work, which gives the twelve-to-one reduction gearing between the minute hand and the hour hand. Very early clocks only had one hand, the hour hand. Obviously, these clocks do not have any motion work.

Having defined the five main subsections, we can now look at how each is arranged within the clock movement.

SIMPLE EIGHT-DAY TIMEPIECE

Power Source

We will assume the power source to be a weight, in keeping with longcase clock tradition, and that the movement is supported on a horizontal board resting across the top of the clock case. This horizontal board is known as the 'seat board' and is usually made from a piece of pine about ¾in (19mm) thick and 4in (100mm) wide and long enough to reach across the top of the trunk section of the clock case where it is supported by the case sides. It is unusual for a seat board to be screwed down to the case sides on antique clocks, although they usually are secured on most reproduction clocks.

The movement sits on the top of the seat board and is held in place by two seat board hooks. These hooks look like miniature walking sticks and the long shaft section is pushed down through drilled holes in the seat board, from above. The holes are so placed that with the movement is in its correct position there will be a hooked end in place to fit over each of the two

lower movement pillars. The shafts are threaded and nuts are screwed on, from below, and tightened to secure the movement firmly in place.

Some clocks do not have seat board hooks, particularly thirty-hour clocks. The movements stay in place due to gravity. The combined weight of the movement, dial, drive weight, doughnut weight and pendulum keeps the underside of the movement in close contact with the seat board. This is perfectly adequate for thirty-hour clocks as the only force used when winding is a straight downward pull on the rope or chain. Eight-day clocks, however, are wound with a cranked key and when winding with this type of key it is possible to dislodge the movement unless it is held firmly in place.

The driving weight is hooked on to an idler pulley. The idler pulley is suspended in a loop of clock line that hangs down below the seat board. One end of the line is passed up through a small drilled hole in the seat board from below, and then knotted at the top to prevent it from pulling back through. The other end goes up through a large slotted hole in the seat board and is attached to the barrel of the clock movement. Here the line is threaded through a hole in the outside diameter of the barrel, close to one end and then knotted on the inside, preventing it from being pulled out.

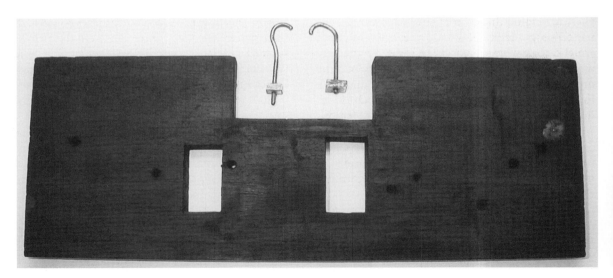

Seat board and hooks.

Movement fitted to the seat board showing layout of line and weights, front plate removed.

By arranging things in this way it is possible to use twice the length of line, for a given drop of the weight, than would be possible if the weight were attached directly to the end of a line wound around the barrel. This is important because during the normal running of an antique clock the line on the barrel will unwind at the rate of one turn every twelve hours.

For an average barrel diameter this would let off roughly 12in (300mm) of line each day. To get eight-days' running time, if the weight were directly attached to the end of the line, would require something like 8ft (2.45m) of clear space between the floor and the underside of the fully wound weight. Add to this the height of the weight and then the hood and pediment of the case, and the overall height of the clock could be somewhere around 11ft (3.4m).

By using an idler pulley, with the end of the line anchored to the seat board in this way, the weight only has to fall 4ft (1.22m) in order to pull off 8ft of line from the barrel.

Eight-day clock lines are available in a variety of different materials. Catgut was traditionally used; now synthetic gut and nylon monofilament line, made under various trade names, is more likely to be used. Rawhide is a natural material, still available and with similar strength to nylon. Bronze and steel braided cable is available; bronze cable is also made with a plastic coating.

The diameter of all these lines is usually 1/16in (1.6mm) for longcase clocks. The strongest material is steel line, but steel, because it is also the hardest of the materials, tends to bite into the surface of the softer brass barrels. This leaves a braided pattern on the barrels which mars the surface finish. Bronze has much less tendency to do this and the plastic-coated bronze, like rawhide and nylon, leaves no marks at all.

For these reasons, steel is usually reserved for three-train movements, particularly the chiming train, where the drive weight is extremely heavy. For standard longcase movements, synthetic gut or nylon line is a good choice, giving ample strength and long life, as well as being the cheapest to buy.

On English-made clocks, the barrel usually has a shallow spiral groove turned around its outside diameter. The groove starts at the drilled hole at one end, where the clock line is knotted in, and runs the full length of the barrel like a screw thread. The purpose of the groove is to guide the line as the clock is wound, so that it winds its way along the barrel in one single thickness with a slight space between each coil. Without the groove the line might bunch up tightly as it is wound, which could cause friction, resulting in a slight loss of power as the line unwinds during normal working.

There should be sixteen full turns of line on a fully wound barrel, which is sufficient to give the clock its eight-day run time. The slot in the seat board, immediately below the barrel, is there to provide clearance for the line as it works its way from one end of the barrel to the other, during normal working and when winding the clock.

Wheel Train

The traditional antique eight-day longcase clock movement has four wheels and three pinions in the going train. We will start with the great wheel, which, as the name suggests, is the largest wheel in the train. The great wheel is fitted on to the barrel arbor and is positioned behind the barrel. It is held against the end of the barrel by a disc of brass, which has a keyhole-shaped cut-out at its centre. This piece is called the 'key plate'.

The round part of the keyhole shape just fits over the barrel arbor and enables the brass disc to be slid on until it is pressing the great wheel against the back of the barrel. In this position the brass disc coincides with a groove machined in the barrel arbor. The groove is wide enough to accept the thickness of the brass disc and deep enough to clear the slotted portion of the keyhole shape. The disc is then moved sideways so that the keyhole slot engages with the groove, thus holding the great wheel in position, but allowing it to turn on the barrel arbor independently of the barrel. The brass disc is prevented from slipping out of the groove by a small screw or pin.

There is a ratchet and pawl device, known as a 'click and ratchet wheel' in horology, acting between the great wheel and the barrel. The click is fitted to the front face of the great wheel and the teeth of the click wheel are machined into the back rim of the barrel. This arrangement ensures that both wheel and barrel turn as a single unit in one direction when the weight is driving the clock, but allows the barrel to be turned in the opposite direction, free of the wheel, when winding the clock.

Groove in the barrel arbor to take key plate.

Great wheel fitted to the barrel arbor.

Key plate fitted over the arbor.

Key plate moved sideways to engage groove in the barrel arbor and pin locking it in place.

Great wheel and barrel assembled, showing click, click spring and ratchet wheel.

The great wheel engages with the centre pinion, which is an integral part of the centre arbor. The centre arbor is the longest arbor in the clock and protrudes right through the front plate of the movement and the dial to drive the minute hand. The centre wheel is riveted to the end of the centre pinion, making the wheel, pinion and arbor assembly one piece. As already mentioned, the minute hand is driven by the centre arbor, therefore the centre arbor must make one complete turn every hour.

The centre wheel engages with and drives the third pinion. The third wheel, which is riveted to the third pinion and arbor making one piece, engages with and drives the escape wheel pinion. The escape wheel, instead of being riveted to its pinion, is mounted on a brass hub called a 'collet', which is positioned approximately mid-way along the length of the arbor. The collet is firmly fixed to the arbor, making the wheel, pinion and arbor a one-piece assembly. There are usually thirty teeth on the escape wheel and these are cut to a special profile, similar to circular saw teeth, instead of the standard gear-tooth profile of the other wheels in the train.

The escape wheel is the last wheel in the train and it makes one full turn every minute. The second hand, if the clock is designed to have one, is driven by the escape wheel arbor, the front pivot of which is made extra long for the purpose. This means that the gearing must drive the escape wheel to make sixty full turns, for every single turn of the centre wheel, there being sixty minutes in one hour.

Barrel, great wheel, centre wheel, third wheel and escape wheel assembled.

Escapement

As already noted, the escape wheel has thirty teeth, therefore the escapement must allow the escape wheel to turn an amount equal to half of one full tooth every second in order to make one full turn in one minute. Strictly speaking, the escapement of any clock would include both the escape wheel and the pallets, as each is designed specifically to work with the other. There have been many different types of escapement designed over the last few hundred years of clock-making. Probably the most common of all, particularly on antique longcase clocks, is the recoil escapement.

At the top of the movement, above the escape wheel, are the pallets. Pallets are referred to in the plural as there are two acting surfaces – one is the entry pallet (sometimes called the outside pallet), and the other is the exit pallet (sometimes called the inside pallet). They are shaped something like the lower curved part of a ship's anchor, but inverted. In fact, this type of escapement is sometimes referred to as an 'anchor escapement'. The pallets are also mounted on an arbor, attached through the centre or belly part of the pallet. The pallet arbor is also a long arbor, but in this case the extra length of the arbor protrudes through the back plate of the clock and is supported by a specially shaped bracket called a 'back cock'.

This arrangement allows a thin wire rod called a 'crutch rod' to be attached at right angles to the

Pallets.

Pallets, back cock and crutch.

pallet arbor, near the back pivot, at the point where the arbor overhangs the back plate. The crutch rod hangs down vertically from the pallet arbor for about 3½in (85mm), just clearing the back plate of the movement. The lower end of the crutch rod is provided with a small steel tab, facing backwards, perpendicular to the back plate. This is called the 'crutch'. The crutch has a rectangular cut-out in it to accept the top block of the pendulum rod. It is of vital importance that the pendulum top block is an easy sliding fit in the crutch. If there is any tendency for the block to bind, this must be corrected as it will certainly have an adverse affect on the performance of the clock and can easily prevent it from working. It is also important to keep this clearance to the bare minimum to prevent lost motion.

The function of the escapement is twofold. Firstly, as already mentioned, it allows the train wheels to run or escape an exact amount at each escaping action. Secondly, it must impart a small restoring impulse to the oscillator, a pendulum in this case. If it were not for this impulse action, given at each beat of the escapement, the effects of gravity would cause the pendulum to gradually lose amplitude until eventually coming to rest.

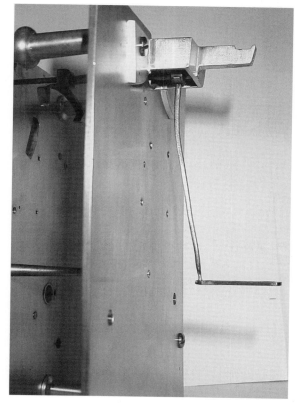

Pallets, back cock and crutch, side view.

As the pendulum swings it causes the pallets to rock from side to side on the pallet arbor, the pallet arbor and pendulum being connected by the crutch. The two pallets are usually spaced so that they enclose seven escape wheel teeth plus half-a-tooth space. Other tooth counts may be found, but, in addition, there is always the odd half-a-tooth space. When any tooth of the escape wheel drops on to either of the two pallets, thus preventing further rotation of the wheel, it is referred to as 'locking'. The ticking sound, associated with clocks, is caused by the escape wheel teeth impinging on to the working surface of the pallets at the locking.

The escapement is so designed that neither pallet can unlock a tooth of the escape wheel until the other is in position ready to lock one of the other teeth. If it were not for this design feature the escapement would 'run through'. As one pallet swings away from the escape wheel, thus releasing a tooth and allowing the escape wheel to turn, the other pallet will have swung into the gap between two adjacent teeth ready for the next tooth to drop on to it and prevent further rotation of the wheel. This ensures that the wheel is only able to turn a distance equal to half-a-tooth space at each beat of the pendulum.

ABOVE LEFT: *Crutch and pendulum top block.*

LEFT: *Pallets and escape wheel showing seven and a half-tooth spaces.*

If the pallets enclosed an exact number of teeth, without the half-a-tooth space, the escape wheel would be unable to turn at all. This is because when one pallet swings away from the escape wheel, to release a tooth, the other pallet swings in towards the wheel and instead of being able to enter a gap, would make contact with one of the other teeth, before the wheel has a chance to turn. There are sixty half-tooth spaces in a thirty-tooth escape wheel and, as most antique longcase clocks have a one-second pendulum beat, the escape wheel will, therefore, make one revolution per minute.

After locking has taken place the pendulum continues to swing a little bit further. This over-swing is referred to as 'supplementary arc', and is necessary to allow for slight manufacturing errors, particularly in the escape wheel. It also provides an allowance for eventual wear in the movement and gradual degradation of the

> ### Number Crunching
>
> It is staggering to think that in a longcase clock, with the pendulum beating seconds, the pallets lock and unlock a tooth on the escape wheel more than thirty-one-and-a-half million times every year. This statistic emphasizes the importance of proper lubrication. Oiling is usually recommended every five years and this equates to almost one hundred and fifty-eight million locking and unlocking actions.

lubricating oils. If the clock were set up for the pendulum to stop swinging at the exact point of unlocking, any one of the above problems might cause a pallet to not quite release the next tooth and the clock would stop.

The acting surfaces of the pallets are so shaped that they form an inclined plane for the escape wheel teeth to slide against. The pallets, being controlled by the pendulum, also continue to

Tooth about to unlock from the entry pallet allowing another tooth to drop onto the exit pallet.

Tooth has dropped and is now locked on the exit pallet.

Tooth at the end of the recoil on the exit pallet.

Tooth at the end of the giving impulse to exit pallet and about to unlock, allowing another tooth to drop onto the entry pallet.

swing a little deeper into engagement with the escape wheel after each locking, due to the supplementary arc of the pendulum. This causes the escape wheel to turn backwards, or recoil, a slight amount, hence the name 'recoil escapement'. The recoiling action can be clearly seen by watching the second hand, if the clock is fitted with one, turn backwards a small amount after each beat of the pendulum.

As the pallets alternately swing away from the escape wheel from the point at which the tooth tip comes to rest after recoil, to the point of unlocking, the escape wheel turns forwards. During this forward movement a tooth tip is pushing the pallet and thus giving impulse to the pendulum. This action can also be clearly seen by looking at the second hand of the clock. After the hand turns backwards a small distance during recoil it will then turn forward a much greater distance, whilst giving impulse to the pendulum. Both the recoil and impulse actions take place slowly and silently.

At the end of impulse, when the acting tooth and pallet unlock, one of the other teeth will drop on to the other pallet and lock the wheel.

Between the unlocking of one tooth and the locking of the next, for a split second, the escape wheel is completely free to rotate. If the second hand is observed it will be seen suddenly speeding up during this period, immediately followed by the tick, as one of the escape wheel teeth impacts on to a pallet at locking. The escapement is the heart of any clock and if badly set up or worn it will have an adverse affect on timekeeping and reliability.

Oscillator

The traditional English longcase clock pendulum is a very simple affair. It consists of a pendulum bob at the bottom, a brass block and suspension spring at the top and a $\frac{1}{8}$in (3mm) diameter pendulum rod joining the two together.

Pendulum top block and suspension spring.

'back cock'. The suspension spring is so called because it is used to suspend the pendulum from the back cock.

In horology, any bracket or support that has only one point of attachment to the movement plate, and therefore gives cantilevered support to any component including pivots, is called a 'cock'. If there is a point of attachment at either side of the point of support it is called a 'bridge'. The back cock on a clock is the odd one out.

The confusion arises because the back cock supports two components simultaneously. It supports the rear pivot of the pallet arbor and has two points of attachment to the movement back plate, one either side of the pallet arbor pivot. This clearly makes it a bridge for the pallet arbor. There is also a rear facing post about 1in (25mm) long, integral with the bridge, and this gives cantilevered support to the pendulum via its suspension spring, making it a cock.

The pendulum rod top block is about ¼in (6mm) wide by ½in (12mm) deep and 1in (25mm) high. The lower end of the top block has a threaded hole into which the pendulum rod is screwed. Across the top surface of the block, from front to back, a narrow vertical slot is made about ⅜in (9mm) deep. Into this slot is fitted the lower end of a thin ribbon of spring steel about 3in (75mm) long and ¼in (6mm) wide, known as the suspension spring.

The suspension spring is held in the block by a pin, riveted into a small hole drilled across the slot, through the brass block and the end of the spring. The uppermost end of the suspension spring has a very much smaller brass block riveted to it in similar fashion. The purpose of the smaller brass block is to prevent the suspension spring from being pulled through a slot in the post used to support it. The post provides cantilevered support to the pendulum and is called a

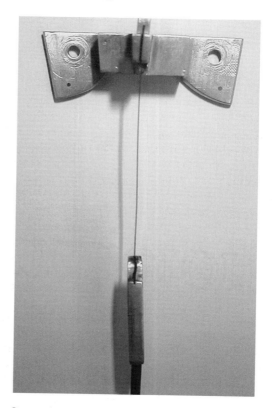

Suspension spring fitted to the back cock, rear view.

The rear-facing post (back cock), when viewed from behind the movement, has a thin vertical slot in it just wide enough to accept the pendulum suspension spring. When the back cock is viewed from the side a notch will be seen running across the top surface, a little way in from its outer end. The small brass block riveted to the top of the pendulum suspension spring will be shaped to fit into the notch, thus preventing the pendulum from moving backwards and slipping off.

Pendulum bobs are usually lenticular in shape, about 4in (100mm) in diameter, and can be made from cast iron or lead. Lead bobs usually have a brass shell, although some have only the front surface faced with brass. When very old lead bobs are found with no brass facing it is probable that the original shell has become detached and lost.

The bottom of the pendulum rod screws into the top end of a narrow strip of steel called a pendulum flat. This is only slightly thicker than the pendulum rod itself and is about ½in (12mm) wide by roughly 4in (100mm) long, and is made a good sliding fit in the bob. The lower end of the pendulum flat is provided with a threaded rod to accept the pendulum rating nut.

The brass top block and pendulum flat are screwed tightly on to the pendulum rod and adjusted until their flat surfaces are at right angles to one another. This arrangement ensures that the pendulum bob swings flat and parallel to the back of the clock case.

The exact length of any pendulum, to give a one-second beat, is dictated by gravity. Geographical location affects the required length of pendulums as gravity varies slightly between the

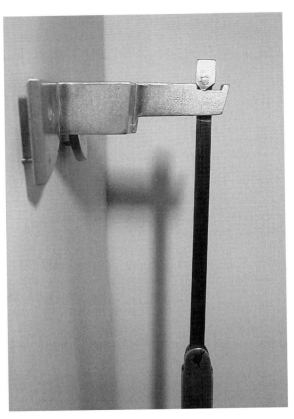

Suspension spring fitted to the back cock, side view.

Pendulum bob.

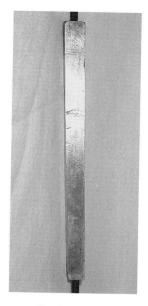

Pendulum flat.

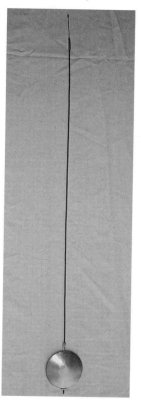

Complete pendulum.

equator and the poles. A pendulum length of 39.14in in London and 39.1in in New York (nominally 1m) will both have a one-second beat. The difference in pendulum length for these two cities is only 0.040in (1mm) and is easily compensated for by adjusting the rating nut. The pendulum lengths quoted above are not the actual overall lengths of the pendulums, but the theoretical lengths, measured between the point of suspension and the centre of oscillation, a point more or less at the centre of the bob.

Motion Work

The motion work on a clock provides the necessary 12:1 reduction gearing between the centre arbor, which drives the minute hand, and the

---

Temperature-Compensated Pendulums

Temperature-compensated pendulums are usually only found on regulators and work as a result of exploiting the different expansion rates of the metals used in their construction. The different metals of the pendulum rod are assembled in such a way that, as they expand or contract due to temperature changes, they cause the pendulum bob automatically to move up or down. This differential expansion maintains the effective length of the pendulum (the distance between the point of suspension and the centre of mass of the bob), thereby ensuring excellent timekeeping.

Steel and brass are the two metals mostly used for these pendulums. A very striking design and probably the most common is known as the 'Harrison gridiron pendulum', named after its inventor John Harrison of 'longitude' fame. The classic layout of a gridiron pendulum is easily recognized by the group of steel and brass rods arranged alternately side by side in a flat grid.

Other designs exist where the pendulum is a single rod made from special steel and all the compensation takes place by virtue of a neat mechanism built into the pendulum bob itself. Mercury is used in some cases, very often seen contained in a large phial on the end of the pendulum rod, in place of a standard metal pendulum bob. Whichever design is used, the manufacturing costs for temperature-compensated pendulums would be significantly greater than for ordinary pendulums.

hour wheel, which drives the hour hand. On traditional English clocks, motion work usually consists of four main components – the cannon pinion, the minute wheel complete with its pinion, the hour bridge complete with pipe, and the hour wheel complete with pipe.

In addition to the 12:1 reduction ratio, provision has to be made for making manual adjustments to the position of the hands when correcting the time. This is achieved by provid-

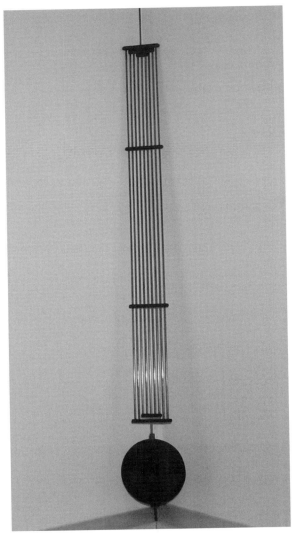

Regulator gridiron pendulum.

ing a friction drive between the centre arbor and the motion work. Without the friction drive, it would be impossible to move the minute hand without breaking something, because the centre arbor is directly geared into the wheel train, and the wheel train, as noted above, is only able to turn as the escapement allows.

The friction drive is provided by the use of a spring called the 'minute friction spring', which is compressed between the back face of the cannon pinion and a shoulder on the centre arbor. The spring consists of a piece of flat springy brass, usually oval in shape, with an overall size of about ½in × ¾in (12 × 19mm). The two ends of the oval are bent up slightly until a gentle curve is formed. A small hole is drilled through the middle of the oval, just large enough to enable it to pass over the centre arbor.

The extended portion of the centre arbor, protruding out through the front plate of the movement, is slightly reduced in diameter to within 0.040in (1mm) of the movement front plate, leaving a small shoulder. The minute spring is fitted over the centre arbor until it butts up against the shoulder with the ends of the spring curving forward, away from the front plate.

The cannon pinion comprises a gear wheel with a long tube (in horology tubes are called pipes) fixed to its centre, instead of an arbor. The centre hole passes right through the wheel and pipe assembly and provides a working fit on the centre arbor. The cannon pinion is fitted on to the centre arbor, until the back face of the pinion presses against the ends of the oval spring.

The front of the cannon has a square drive, matched to fit the square hole in the boss of the minute hand. The minute hand is retained, on the squared end of the cannon, by a special dome-shaped washer, approximately ½in (12mm) diameter, called a 'hand collet'. The hand collet is slipped over the end of the centre arbor and pushed on hard. The hand collet presses against the outer surface of the minute hand which, in turn, is held tightly on to the squared end of the cannon.

The cannon is pushed back on the centre arbor, compressing the oval spring between the shoulder on the centre arbor and the back of the cannon pinion. When the hand collet is held in this position a small diameter cross hole will be revealed at the tip of the centre arbor. A tapered pin fitted into the cross hole holds the assembly together, with the spring in the compressed state.

The minute hand, because it is connected by a square drive to the cannon, cannot be turned

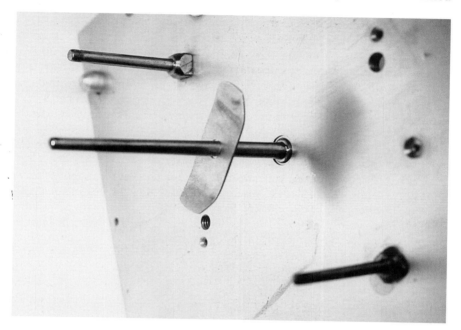

Centre arbor and minute tension spring.

Cannon and pipe, showing square drive for the minute hand.

without turning the cannon pinion and vice versa. The oval spring, held in compression, provides sufficient friction to drive the cannon pinion, together with the minute hand, round as one with the centre arbor when the clock is working normally. It also enables the minute hand to be moved backwards or forwards when manually setting the clock to the correct time. In this example, the friction takes place between the shoulder on the centre arbor and the small area it bears against at the back of the minute spring.

On some clocks the hole in the minute spring is made square and a mating square is provided immediately in front of the shoulder of the centre arbor. This arrangement creates a more positive drive. The minute spring cannot rotate on the centre arbor because of the mating squares, therefore, when the minute hand is manually

Minute wheel.

Minute tension spring, cannon, minute hand, hand collet and pin assembled on the centre arbor.

Hour wheel (with snail fitted).

Hour bridge fitted over the cannon pinion and the centre arbor.

adjusted, the back face of the cannon pinion is made to slip against the outer ends of the minute spring. The same frictional resistance, acting at a much greater radius, gives a more positive drive.

The cannon pinion engages with and drives the minute wheel. The minute wheel is riveted on to one end of the minute pinion. The pinion has a hole through its full length and the wheel and pinion assembly rotates on a post, screwed into the movement front plate. The minute wheel is positioned nearest to the movement plate, with its pinion to the front where it engages with and drives the hour wheel.

Hour wheel fitted to the hour bridge.

The hour wheel has a pipe attached to it, the 'hour pipe', which is quite short and stout, its outer end being machined to accept the boss of the hour hand. The hour wheel and pipe assembly fits over yet another pipe, the 'hour bridge pipe', projecting from the centre of the hour bridge. The hour bridge is secured to the front plate and positioned so that its pipe fits concentrically over the centre arbor and cannon.

The hour bridge, with its pipe, is designed to give robust support to the hour wheel and pipe assembly. The bore of the hour bridge pipe is greater than the outside diameter of the cannon, therefore the centre arbor and cannon are not subjected to any side loading. They can rotate without having to do anything more than drive the minute wheel round and carry the minute hand.

The cannon pinion and the minute wheel have the same number of teeth, and so being meshed together they will both rotate at the same speed. The minute hand, cannon pinion and centre arbor will all turn in unison and in a clockwise direction. The minute wheel, together with its pinion, will be driven in an anti-clockwise direction.

The minute wheel pinion has six teeth (in horology pinion teeth are called 'leaves') and meshes with the hour wheel, which has seventy-two teeth. This means that the minute wheel and pinion assembly, with the centre arbor and cannon, will have to rotate twelve times to drive the hour wheel round once. The hour wheel is driven in a clockwise direction.

Cannon and minute wheel fitted.

5 THE STRIKE TRAIN AND HOW IT WORKS

The two systems commonly used are the rack strike and the count wheel strike (sometimes referred to as locking wheel or locking plate strike). Both eight-day and thirty-hour clocks can be found using either system. Thirty-hour clocks differ from eight-day clocks in their wheel train layout. There is, however, little difference in the wheel train layout of a rack strike or count wheel strike clock of the same running duration.

The rack strike is the later of the two types, with the key difference between them being the way in which the hammer blows to the bell are counted by the mechanism so as to strike the correct hour. There are many design variations found for both systems, but the following descriptions will deal with a typical eight-day rack strike and a thirty-hour count wheel strike.

EIGHT-DAY RACK STRIKE

Strike Train

There are four wheels and four pinions in the strike train, all very similar to the going train, except that none of the wheels in the strike train acts as an escape wheel. Following on from the great wheel, there is the pin wheel, then the third wheel and finally the warning wheel.

There is one more vital component, situated at the end of the strike train, called 'the fly'. The fly is little more than a flat rectangular piece of brass sheet mounted on an arbor. The arbor is made with an integral pinion. Because it is situated at the end of the train it revolves at quite a high speed when the train is released to strike the hours. Being a flat rectangular shape and rotating at speed, the fly fans the air and acts as an air

brake or governor. This ensures that the strike train cannot race away but will run at a steady speed giving a regular strike.

The strike train great wheel fits on its barrel arbor, with a click and ratchet wheel and a brass retaining disc, exactly as for the time train described in Chapter Four. The great wheel engages with and drives the pin wheel pinion.

Complete eight-day strike train including hammer and spring.

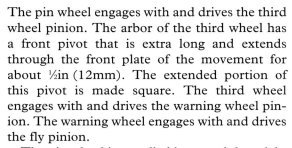

Hammer, hammer spring, pin wheel and bell.

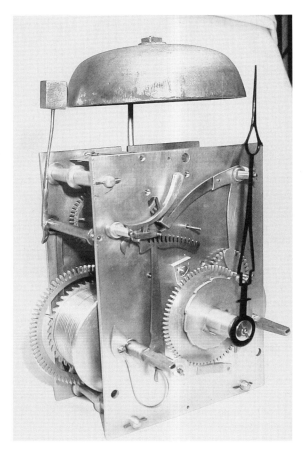

Complete movement with bell fitted.

The pin wheel engages with and drives the third wheel pinion. The arbor of the third wheel has a front pivot that is extra long and extends through the front plate of the movement for about ½in (12mm). The extended portion of this pivot is made square. The third wheel engages with and drives the warning wheel pinion. The warning wheel engages with and drives the fly pinion.

The pin wheel is so called because it has eight short pins riveted into its outer face. These are evenly spaced in a pitch circle around the rim of the wheel and stand out at right angles to its front face. The warning wheel has a single pin fitted into its rim in the same way. There is another arbor mounted between the movement plates,

positioned just over halfway up and close to the outer edge. It is called the 'hammer arbor' and although essential to the strike mechanism it does not form part of the strike train.

At the rear end of the hammer arbor, and attached at a tangent to it, is a thin rod about 3in (75mm) long, called the 'hammer arm', which carries the hammer head. The hammer arm stands up vertically at the side of the movement when the hammer arbor is at rest. The hammer head, at the top of the arm, is in line with the rim of a bell which is usually about 4in (100mm) diameter.

The bell is mounted on a central post at the top of the movement and covers the mechanism rather like an umbrella. The bottom of the hammer arm, where it attaches to the hammer arbor, projects downwards for about ¼in (6mm) past the arbor, forming a tail called the 'hammer tail'. The area beneath the arbor, at this point of attachment, is provided with a flat pad forming a right angle with the hammer tail.

One end of a stout 3in (75mm) long leaf spring is attached vertically to the bottom inside surface of the back plate, below the position of the hammer arbor. The top of the leaf spring is bent over to form an inverted 'L' shape. The spring is attached to the plate in such a way that its inverted 'L'-shaped top fits into the right angle formed by the hammer tail and flat pad, on the underside of the hammer arbor.

The tip of the inverted 'L' holds a spring tension against the hammer tail tending to rotate the arbor on its pivots, pushing the hammer head towards the bell. This causes the flat pad on the underside of the hammer arbor to lock firmly against the top surface of the leaf spring, forming a positive stop.

By this simple design two essential functions are performed with the minimum number of parts. First, the hammer arbor is able to turn in one direction, against the tension of the leaf spring, so that when released it can fly back and the hammer will strike the bell. Second, the hammer arbor is locked firmly on its stop, with the hammer in the upright position after each hammer blow.

There is one more arm about 1in (25mm) long attached to the front end of the hammer arbor and radial to it. This arm is positioned so that it projects into the narrow space between the outer face of the pin wheel and the front plate of the movement. This arm is also referred to, in some reference books, as the 'hammer tail'. The reason for the confusion is due to the way clock movements have evolved over the centuries.

The change from birdcage to plated movement design meant that the long hammer tail had to be moved from the middle, to one end of its arbor, to operate with the pin wheel. This resulted in the need for a short tail, below the hammer arm, to act with the leaf spring at the other end. To avoid further confusion, this second arm will be referred to as the 'hammer lifting tail' from here on.

With the strike train locked at rest, the tip of the hammer lifting tail just projects into the area between two adjacent pins in the pin wheel. When the strike train runs and the pin wheel rotates, each pin in turn comes around to engage with and lift the tip of the tail. This in turn cocks the hammer back against its spring.

As the wheel turns a little further the pin moves past the tip of the tail and releases it. The hammer immediately flies back to its original position, under the influence of the leaf spring, until the hammer arbor butts on its stop (the flat top of the leaf spring) and comes to rest suddenly. Due to momentum, the hammer head continues to move forwards, causing the hammer arm, supporting it, to flex slightly, resulting in the bell being struck. The tip of the hammer lifting tail is

Hammer at rest, train locked.

Pin contacting the hammer lifting tail.

Hammer fully cocked, about to strike.

then back in position, between two adjacent pins on the pin wheel, ready to be lifted by another pin and strike the next hammer blow to the bell.

Hour-Counting Mechanism, Strike Release and Run-to-Warning Mechanism

Every part of the strike train is fitted inside the movement, between the front and back plates. The strike train is controlled by various components mounted on to the front surface of the front plate. These components are sometimes collectively referred to as 'under-dial work'.

Antique longcase clocks are usually made to strike the hours only and do not strike at the half hour at all. For ease of explanation, the various components of the strike mechanism are best divided into two sections. One section counts the

number of hammer blows struck and then locks the train ready for the next hour, and the other section releases the strike train on the hour.

Hour-Counting Mechanism

There are five main components in this section – the rack, the rack hook, the rack spring, the gathering pallet and the hour snail. The rack is made from steel and is 'T' shaped. There is a brass boss (pipe), one end of which is riveted into a large hole at the bottom of the upright leg of the 'T'. The pipe fits over a post, which is screwed into the movement front plate, thus enabling the rack to pivot to the left or right when viewed from the front of the movement.

When fitted to the post, the rack is positioned closest to the movement front plate, with the pipe

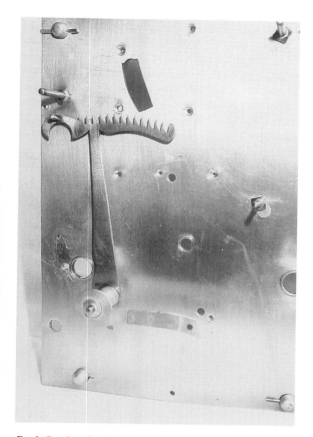

Rack fitted to the front plate.

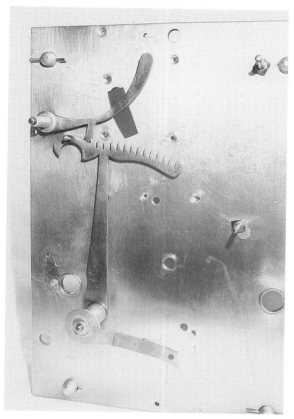

Rack hook fitted to the front plate.

to the front. The top surface of the upper cross member of the 'T' is at a radius to the pivot point and is provided with a number of saw-like teeth. Fitted at the front of this toothed section at the extreme left-hand side (when viewed from the front) is a short pin. There is also a thin arm, which is usually made from brass, riveted on to the front end of the rack pipe projecting out to the right at an angle of about 90 degrees to the upright leg of the 'T'. This piece is called the 'rack tail'. The rack tail has a short steel peg called a 'beak' riveted on to its extreme end and perpendicular to its back face.

The rack hook is made from steel and is a long curved arm with a pipe at one end and a single tooth protruding from its curved underside, roughly midway along its length. The rack spring is usually made from brass wire formed into a 'U'

Rack spring.

shape. The end of one leg of the 'U' has a mounting pad, called a 'foot', for fixing it to the front plate. The other end acts on the rack, close to the pivot point. The diameter of the wire used to make the rack spring is gradually tapered down from the mounting foot end to the rack end. Using a long tapered spring gives an even tension to the rack over its full range of travel, from the one o'clock to the twelve o'clock position.

Gathering pallet.

Hour snail.

The gathering pallet, again made from steel, is a short, single-tooth pinion with a square hole lengthways through it. At the front of the pinion, projecting out to the side opposite the single tooth, is a long tail. The gathering pallet is fitted on to the squared end of the third wheel arbor, where it is held in place by a tapered pin passed through a small cross hole in the extreme end of the arbor.

The hour snail is made from sheet brass. It is called a snail because its profile resembles a snail's shell. The snail starts life as a round disc approximately 1½in (38mm) in diameter with a hole in the middle so that it can be fitted over the hour wheel pipe. The disc is marked off into twelve 30 degree sectors. The first segment is kept at the original radius from its centre, but each successive

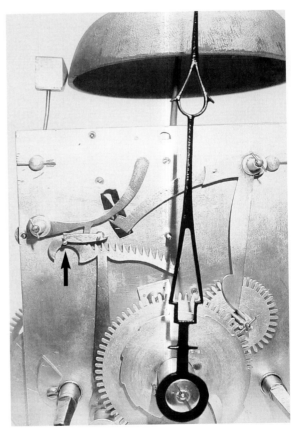

Front view of assembled clock, gathering pallet tail locked on rack pin.

30 degree sector is stepped down to a smaller radius. From the first sector to the last there are twelve equal steps, one for each hour.

The hour snail is the component that dictates how many hammer blows are struck after the strike train has been released, by limiting the depth the rack tail can fall. It is the very fact that the hour snail is driven independently from the strike train that makes rack striking so different from count wheel striking. The hour snail is attached to, and driven by, the hour wheel of the motion work; the motion work, of course, is driven by the time train. This means that a clock fitted with rack striking, assuming it is not badly worn or maladjusted, can only strike the correct number of times as indicated by the hour hand of the clock.

When at rest, the strike train is prevented from running because the end of the gathering pallet tail is locked against the short pin, fitted to the front left-hand side of the toothed section of the rack. The rack is locked in place by the rack hook engaging with the last tooth on the rack.

Strike Release and Run-to-Warning Mechanism
The strike release and run-to-warning mechanism consists of only one main component, made up from two arms riveted together on a pipe, in inverted 'V' formation. The axis of the pipe is at right angles to the plane of the 'V', enabling the two arms to pivot on a post, set high up to the right of the movement front plate.

When viewed from the front, one arm of the 'V' projects down, at a slight angle to the vertical, with its tip positioned just in front of the minute wheel, but not long enough to reach the minute pinion. This arm is called the 'lifting piece' and is usually made from brass. The other arm goes horizontally across the front plate towards the left-hand side; this arm is called the 'warning piece' and is made from steel.

The position of the end of the warning piece arm, in front of the movement plate, coincides with the position of the warning wheel behind the plate. The front plate, at this point, has a cut-out in it to enable a projection fixed to the back of the warning piece to go through the plate, almost up to the face of the warning wheel. The warning

piece is sturdily made and because, when at rest, it is in the horizontal position the end will always fall to the bottom of the cut-out in the front plate due to gravity.

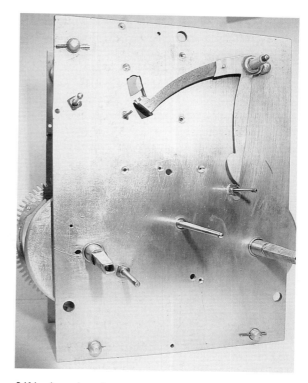

Lifting/warning piece.

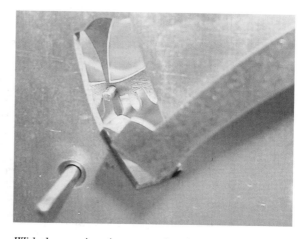

With the warning piece at rest the pin on the warning wheel just clears, allowing the train to run.

How it Works The minute wheel has a pin inserted into its front face, and as the wheel rotates the pin comes round and makes contact with the end of the lifting piece. As the minute wheel continues turning, the pin pushes the lifting piece to the left. Because the two arms are riveted together on their pipe, this has the effect of lifting the warning piece. The top surface of the warning piece, as it continues to lift, makes contact with the underside of the rack hook.

When the rack hook has been lifted high enough, at about five minutes or so before each hour, it will release the rack. Once released, the rack is free to pivot on its post, assisted by the rack spring, until the beak, riveted to the end of the rack tail, makes contact with one of the steps on the hour snail. Pressure from the rack spring holds the beak in close contact with the snail.

As the rack is released, the pin fitted to the front left of the rack teeth releases the tail on the gathering pallet, which in turn releases the strike train. Once released, the strike train starts to run, but is quickly halted by the pin in the warning wheel coming into contact with the projection at the back of the warning piece. This sequence of events is indicated by a clunking sound, as the rack tail beak strikes the hour snail, followed by a whirring sound as the train begins to run. This very brief period of running is referred to as the 'run to warning'.

Just as the minute hand reaches the hour position, the pin on the minute wheel just moves past the end of the lifting piece, thus releasing it. Gravity then causes the warning lever to drop to the bottom of its cut-out, clear of the pin in the warning wheel, and the train is free to run.

Minute wheel pin contacting lifting piece.

Warning piece making contact with the rack hook.

*Rack hook releases rack,
rack tail beak contacts hour
snail, strike train held on
the warning.*

*Minute wheel pin releases
the lifting piece on the hour.
The warning piece falls,
releasing the warning wheel
and the strike train runs.*

As the train runs, the gathering pallet rotates, and gathers up the rack teeth at the rate of one tooth per revolution. The third wheel arbor, carrying the gathering pallet, is geared at a ratio of 8:1 with the pin wheel. This means that for every revolution of the third wheel, and therefore the gathering pallet, one tooth of the rack is gathered and one of the eight pins in the pin wheel will cause the hammer to strike one blow on the bell.

The rack hook is positioned so that its single tooth will latch over each tooth on the rack as it is gathered. This prevents the rack from springing back, under the influence of the rack spring, when the gathering pallet rotates to a position where its single tooth becomes disengaged from the rack teeth. When the last tooth on the rack has been gathered up, the rack hook locks the rack in position. The tail on the gathering pallet comes into contact with, and is locked once more by, the pin fitted to the front left of the toothed section of the rack.

LEFT: *Gathering pallet gathering up the rack.*

Rack hook drops behind a tooth, locking the rack, before the gathering pallet tooth disengages.

THIRTY-HOUR COUNT WHEEL STRIKE

Strike Train

There are only three wheels and two pinions in a thirty-hour strike train plus the fly. It is the pin wheel and pinion, used in eight-day wheel trains, which is dispensed with. Instead of having a separate pin wheel, the pins are fitted to the great wheel. The hammer tail is lifted by the pins in the usual way. Due to the absence of the pin wheel, it is the pinion of the third wheel which is driven by the great wheel. It can no longer be called a third wheel, however, because in thirty-hour clocks it is only the second wheel after the great wheel.

Hoop wheel.

This second wheel is actually called a 'hoop wheel'. The name derives from the hoop- or ring-shaped piece that forms an integral part of the front face of the wheel. A small segment of the hoop is cut away so that it does not form a continuous ring. The gear ratio between the hoop wheel pinion and the great wheel is such that one pin in the great wheel will lift and release the hammer tail for each complete revolution of the hoop wheel.

There is one extra arbor needed in a count wheel striking movement and it is positioned to one side of the plates, just above the hammer arbor, and it is called the 'locking detent arbor' or 'detent arbor'. The locking detent arbor is positioned in line with the top of the hoop wheel. Integral with this arbor, and at a radius to it, is a stout arm long enough to reach across and rest on the top of the hoop wheel. This arm is called the 'hoop wheel detent' or 'locking piece'. The end of the hoop wheel detent reaches as far as the vertical centreline of the hoop wheel. A projection on the underside of the extreme end of the detent, locates in the cut-out of the hoop, locks the wheel and prevents the strike train from running.

Thirty-hour strike train assembled in the back plate.

Locking detent arbor, detent shown locking the hoop wheel.

Count wheel and its detent shown assembled on the back plate.

Hour-Counting Mechanism

There are only two components used for counting the hours with count wheel striking. The first is the count wheel and the second is the count wheel detent. In later clocks the count wheel is made from a brass casting shaped something like a top hat, with a very short top. The gear teeth are cut in the brim of the top hat section and the tube part acts as the count wheel.

The count wheel has a hole through its centre and is mounted on a post, which is screwed into the movement back plate. The tube part of the wheel is positioned nearest to the movement back plate. It is retained in position, on the post, by a triangular brass spring plate, which also has a hole through it to match the diameter of the post. The spring plate is held, under tension, against the wheel by a tapered pin passed through a hole drilled across the end of the post. The count wheel is able to turn on the post and is driven by a pinion fitted to an extension of the great wheel arbor.

In any twelve-hour period there are seventy-eight hammer blows struck on the bell. This is the sum total of all the hours struck by the clock, successively, from one o'clock through to twelve o'clock. The count wheel is divided up into seventy-eight sectors, each sector representing one hammer blow. Twelve of the count wheel sectors are notched out. These notches mark the last hammer blow for each of the twelve-hour counts. When the strike train is running, as each pin in the great wheel lifts and releases the hammer tail, the pinion on the great wheel arbor will turn the count wheel by an amount equal to one sector.

The count wheel detent is an arm about 2in (50mm) long with a square hole at one end. This fits over the squared end of the extended pivot at the rear of the locking detent arbor. The count wheel detent is held out horizontally, across the back plate of the movement. The very end of this detent is bent down at a right angle and is able to locate in the notches on the count wheel. The front pivot of the locking detent arbor is also extended and is squared at the end, where it projects through the front plate of the movement. Fitted to the square is another horizontal arm,

the 'locking detent lifting arm', which looks very much like the rack hook, described in the previous section, except that it is minus the single tooth on its underside. The locking detent lifting arm and both detents are rigidly secured to the locking detent arbor, none being able to rise or fall independently. When the lifting arm is lifted, both detents are simultaneously lifted until clear of their respective wheels.

Strike Release and Run-to-Warning Mechanism

The lifting piece and warning piece assembly is very similar to that already described for an eight-day clock. The main difference is that the assembly is pivoted on the left-hand side of the movement front plate and the pin which operates the lifting piece is fitted to the cannon pinion and not the minute wheel.

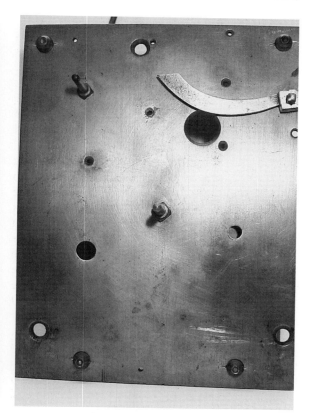

Locking detent lifting arm.

Pin fitted to thirty-hour cannon pinion.

How it Works

When the strike train is locked, the locking detent lifting arm is horizontal and its end is positioned just above the end of the warning piece. As the cannon pinion turns, its pin lifts the lifting piece, which, in turn, causes the warning piece to lift.

The top of the warning piece contacts the underside of the lifting arm and, as the cannon pinion continues turning, the lifting arm is raised until the train is unlocked and the strike train runs to warning. On the hour, the pin on the cannon pinion moves past the tip of the lifting piece, allowing it to drop back, together with the warning piece, to release the train to strike the hours. Each time the hoop wheel makes one revolution the clock will strike once.

Let us assume the clock has just finished striking twelve o'clock. The tip of the count wheel detent is in the notch, on the count wheel, marking the end of the twelve o'clock strike and the locking detent is engaged in the cut-out on the hoop wheel, locking the train. On the hour of one o'clock, the lifting piece is released by the pin on the cannon pinion, which causes the warning piece

to release the strike train. The hoop wheel makes one revolution, causing the hammer to strike the bell once. The count wheel has also been moved on one sector, which happens to be another notch, to mark the end of the one o'clock strike. At this point, the cut-out in the hoop and the notch in the count wheel are in position to allow both detents to drop into place, and the train is locked.

Because one o'clock needs only a single strike, it will also be the last strike for that hour, therefore that sector on the count wheel has to be a notch. This follows directly after the notch marking the end of the twelve o'clock strike and gives us two notches side by side, which, at first glance, might be mistaken for a single extra-wide notch.

On the hour of two o'clock, when the train is released, the hoop wheel makes one revolution

Thirty-hour lifting/warning piece on the front plate.

Warning piece contacting the detent lifting arm.

Position of arms and levers at the run to warning.

Count wheel and locking detent lifted clear of their wheels at the run to warning.

and the first blow to the bell is struck. The count wheel is also moved on one sector, but because it is not the last strike for that hour there is no notch. Therefore, the tip of the count wheel detent touches the full diameter of the count wheel and this prevents the locking detent from dropping into the cut-out on the hoop and locking the train. The hoop wheel is free to make another revolution and the second, and final, blow to the bell is struck. The count wheel is also moved on one sector, and because this is the last sector for that hour, it is notched, allowing both detents to drop into place and lock the train.

This sequence of events is repeated up until the twelve o'clock position, with each successive hour having one more full diameter sector than

The two notches, side by side, on the count wheel.

Count wheel detent shown in position, following the first strike for two o'clock.

The locking detent is unable to enter and lock the hoop wheel because the count wheel detent holds it clear.

its predecessor. Because the lifting arm and both detents are on the same side of the detent arbor, gravity will cause the detents to drop in and lock the train when any one of the notches in the count wheel permits.

VARIATIONS

The above descriptions are fairly typical and will apply to the majority of clocks. Once the purpose of each component, and the sequence of operations between them, is properly understood there will be no trouble in understanding how other designs work.

The count wheel described above is typical of later clocks. There are other designs, usually comprising of two separate wheels, the count wheel and drive wheel, riveted together with a narrow spacer between them. Some, however, instead of having a notched wheel, have twelve pins fitted into the face of a wheel that are spaced to mark the last strike in each hour count. In this case, changes will have been made to the locking arrangements, because locking takes place when the locking detent arbor is lifted by any one of the pins.

Thirty-Hour Rack Strike

A thirty-hour rack strike movement has the rack and all associated components on the front plate, exactly as described above for the eight-day rack strike. A standard type of locking wheel, with extended front pivot and gathering pallet, will be found in place of the hoop wheel. The locking detent arbor, complete with detents, and the count wheel, together with its driving pinion, will not be present.

Eight-Day Count Wheel Strike

A hoop wheel will be found in place of the usual third wheel and gathering pallet. A locking detent arbor, complete with two detents and lifting arm, will be situated just above the hammer arbor. A count wheel will be found mounted on the back plate, and a pinion to drive it. Eight-day movements have the count wheel driving pinion mounted on an extension to the pin wheel arbor, whereas in thirty-hour movements it is mounted on an extension to the great wheel arbor. This is because, in eight-day movements, the hoop wheel pinion is driven by the pin wheel and not the great wheel. The gear ratio between the pin wheel and the hoop wheel allows one hammer blow to the bell per complete revolution of the hoop wheel.

Sometimes, eight-day count wheel strike clocks are found where there is no count wheel mounted on the back plate at all. Instead, it is mounted on the strike train great wheel. The count wheel, in any clock, must make one complete revolution in twelve hours. We know that the great wheel, in eight-day clocks, also turns once in twelve hours, as discussed at the beginning of Chapter Four. Therefore, it makes sense to mount the count wheel directly on to the great wheel and save the complication and expense of providing a separate drive system. This method is known as 'inside count wheel strike'.

COMMON PROBLEMS WITH COUNT WHEEL CLOCKS

Unlike rack striking, which is controlled by the time train (hour snail), count wheel striking is a purely sequential system. Whenever the clock strikes, it can only strike the hour count following

on from the one previously struck. This it will do irrespective of the hour indicated by the hands of the clock.

When correctly set up, the hour indicated by the hour hand and the number of hours struck on the bell are synchronized. Providing the movement is not badly worn or maladjusted, and it is wound regularly at the correct interval, it should strike without problem for many years. Sometimes, however, when the mechanism becomes very worn, there can be a tendency to mis-lock at the end of a strike.

When this happens, the clock will continue to strike the next hour count without pause. Each time this happens, any future striking will be one greater than the hour indicated by the hands. For example, if the clock were striking correctly in the morning, and it then mis-locked three

Eight-day inside count wheel.

times during the course of the day, at nine o'clock in the evening it would strike twelve times. Then, at ten o'clock, it would strike the next number in sequence, which, of course, is one.

Even with a movement in good condition and receiving proper maintenance there are two very common causes for the strike to get out of synchronization with the hands. The first, and most likely cause, with eight-day clocks is failing to wind the clock before the end of its running duration. Very often the strike train will run down before the time train. When this happens, the hour indicated by the hands will move on some hours ahead of the last hour struck. Therefore, when the clock is wound, the striking will resume with the next hour count in the sequence and this is likely to give fewer strikes than the hour indicated by the hands.

Thirty-hour clocks only have one weight and if the clock is allowed to become fully wound down both the strike and time trains stop together. On winding, the clock will carry on where it left off.

If a pendulum clock, with count wheel striking, is to be left unattended for a period of time greater than its running duration, it is best to stop it before leaving. Once returned, it is a simple matter to start the pendulum swinging, at the point when the actual time coincides with that indicated by the hands of the clock. This will avoid the problem of having to correct the strike and wind the hands around to the correct time. If the hands are moved forwards, it is very important that the hour is allowed to strike fully before moving on to the next hour. If this is not done, the strike will automatically go out of synchronization.

The second most common cause of this problem is moving the minute hand back to correct the time after the clock has run to warning. When the train is held on the warning pin, moving the minute hand back will allow the lifting piece, and because they are joined together the warning piece as well, to move back, thus releasing the train. When the minute hand comes back up to the hour again it will let the next strike sequence

go and will now, of course, be one hour out. This is, in fact, the easiest way for the owner to get the clock back in synchronization if it does strike incorrectly. It may mean letting the strike off in this way for perhaps as many as eleven times before it is corrected.

If the clock is fast and the minute hand does need to be moved back, it is best to do it during the first half hour, after the clock has struck. The golden rule, always to be observed, is never, under any circumstances, move the minute hand back through the hour position. At the hour the lifting piece drops off the pin, fitted to the minute wheel, or the cannon in the case of thirty-hour clocks. If the minute hand is turned back at this time, the wheel and pin turn backwards and the pin will make contact with the opposite side of the lifting piece. The lifting

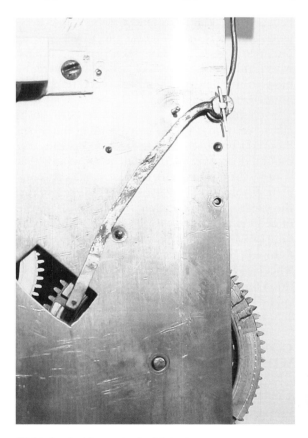

Eight-day inside count wheel detent.

piece is prevented from moving backwards because the end of the warning piece is resting on the bottom of the cut-out in the front plate. Forcing the minute hand back through the hour will cause something to break, or at the very least to be bent out of shape.

Some clocks have a specially shaped end to the lifting piece and a chamfer on the back of the pin. The lifting piece is also made of thin, springy brass and, if the hand is turned backwards, the chamfer on the back of the pin causes the lifting piece to spring to the side and allows the pin to pass. Once the pin has passed, the lifting piece springs back to its original position with no ill effects to the clock. However, it is probably best to be safe rather than sorry and not to rely on this refinement, even if it is known to exist on your clock.

6 THE RESTORATION PROJECT

Once you have bought your clock you must first assess its condition, ascertain as much as possible about its history, and establish what repairs and restoration are needed. It is best to treat separately each of the three main components – the case, the dial and hands, and the movement. You may require the help of a professional horologist to do this. The clock used for the restoration project described in this book was purchased privately following a chance remark made to its previous owner.

The clock had not worked for many years and was in a sad state, as can be seen from the photographs. The case is mahogany, in the London style, with scalloped pediment, three ball and spire finials and bracket feet, standing 7ft 5in (2.25m) high to the top of the centre spire. The dial is a 12in (30cm) painted break-arch with Arabic numerals. The movement is a standard eight-day, rack striking on a 4½in (114mm) diameter cast bell. All the indications are that the clock dates from the beginning of the nineteenth century. During the course of the restoration evidence may be found which will tie the date down more accurately.

Fortunately, the clock was complete and appeared to be original, with no signs of any major botched repairs. The case had suffered from the natural effects of the wood drying out and shrinking. Because a clock case is constructed in a box-like fashion, it is inevitable that some of the wood grain will be running in different directions, and so as the wood dries out and shrinks, stresses are set up within the structure.

The stressing is caused mainly because the wood shrinks by a greater amount across the grain than it does in line with the grain. Also, if a case is made up of more than one type of wood, or has been veneered, each may shrink at a different rate. As the stresses build up, a point is reached when the weakest component will give way. The end result is joints that are pulled apart, or cracks and splits appearing in the wood – in fact, usually a combination of both. Because the

Clock shown, as found.

glue used in all antique furniture, including clock cases, was made from animal by-products it too will deteriorate with age. This will also cause loose joints and pieces of moulding and veneer to come loose or fall off.

ASSESSING THE THREE MAIN COMPONENTS OF THE PROJECT CLOCK

Case
We will start at the plinth and work towards the top of the clock. The plinth on this clock is not original; although made from mahogany with a good colour match, the wood used and its method

of construction is different from that of the rest of the case. It was probably replaced during the late nineteenth or early twentieth century.

The profile at the bottom front of the plinth, giving the bracket feet, is very roughly cut and poorly proportioned. There is a tide mark, clearly visible in the photographs, running around the base almost halfway between the top of the plinth and the bottom of the front panel moulding. This mark indicates the probable position of the top of the original plinth. If this were the case, the proportions would then be correct as the border between the front panel moulding and the sides would equal that between the panel moulding and the top of the plinth.

Plinth shown from the left.

Plinth shown from the right.

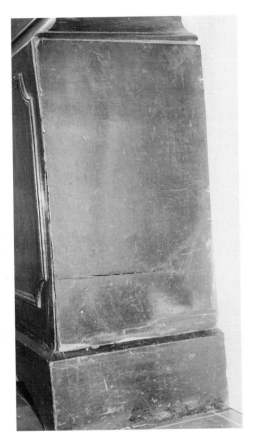

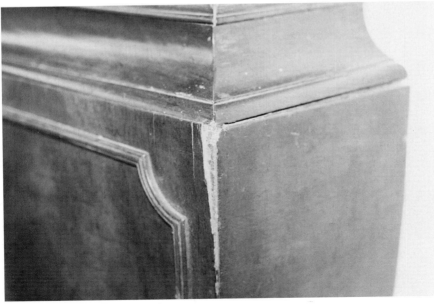

ABOVE LEFT: Splits and missing veneer to the right side of the base.

ABOVE RIGHT: Split in the door.

LEFT: Missing veneer at the top right of base.

ABOVE: George Barrett, Stowmarket.
RIGHT: John Smith, Pittenweem.
BELOW: Simms, Chipping Norton.
BELOW RIGHT: W. Urie, Dundee.

LEFT: *Scott, Dunning.*
ABOVE: *Barwife, Cockermouth.*

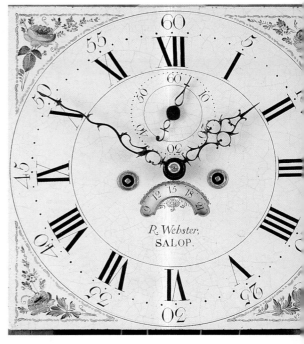

LEFT: *J. Richardson, Easingwold.*
ABOVE: *R. Webster, Salop.*

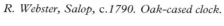
R. Webster, Salop, c.1790. Oak-cased clock.

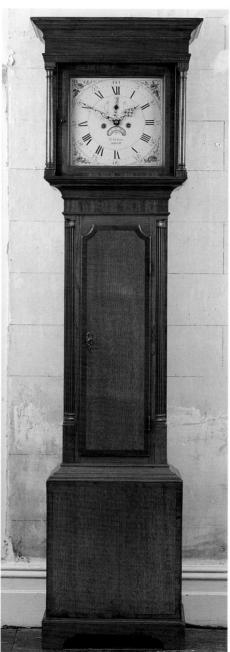

J. Barber, Winster, c.1720. An eight-day clock with an oak case. Early unnumbered.

Monkhouse, Carlisle, c.1790. A thirty-hour clock with an oak and mahogany case.

LEFT: Holliwell & Son, Derby (left clock) and M. Parker, Dunfermline (right clock).
BELOW: J. Knight, Riverhead.

J. Knight, Riverhead.

J. Smith, Pittenweem.

W. Urie, Dundee.

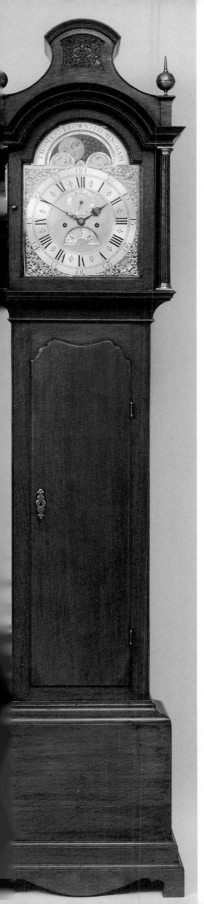

LEFT: *T. Brown, Birmingham.*

RIGHT: *J. Smith, Pittenweem.*

BELOW LEFT: *Simms, Chipping Norton. A thirty-hour, single-handed clock with an oak case.*

BELOW RIGHT: *G. Peacock, London, c.1795. An eight-day clock with a mahogany case.*

*LEFT: J. Durward,
Edinburgh,* c.*1800.
Mahogany-cased clock.*

*RIGHT: R. Kenfield,
Winchester,* c.*1795.
Mahogany-cased clock.*

*RIGHT: A. Barber,
Bristol,* c.*1795.
Mahogany-cased clock.*

*LEFT: J. Chambley,
Wolverhampton,* c.*1780.
An eight-day clock with an
oak and mahogany case.*

*RIGHT: R. Beveridge,
Newburgh,* c.*1795.
Mahogany-cased clock.*

LEFT: *Stansbury, Bromyard, c.1720. An eight-day clock with an oak case.*

RIGHT: *Yardley, Bishop Stortford, late eighteenth century. An eight-day clock with an oak case.*

BELOW: *J. Barber, Winster, c.1762. A thirty-hour clock, numbered 593 with an oak case.*

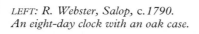

LEFT: *R. Webster, Salop, c.1790. An eight-day clock with an oak case.*

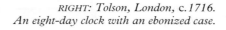

RIGHT: *Tolson, London, c.1716. An eight-day clock with an ebonized case.*

LEFT: J. Barber, Winster, c.1755. A thirty-hour clock with an oak case, numbered 271.

RIGHT: R. Edgar, Whitehaven, c.1830. An eight-day wall clock with a mahogany case.

RIGHT: J. Sharman, Melton Mowbray, c.1805. An eight-day clock with an oak case.

LEFT: Monkhouse, Carlisle, c.1790. A thirty-hour clock with an oak and mahogany case.

LEFT: Ogden, Halifax, c.1750. An eight-day clock with spherical ball moon phase and a lacquer case.

RIGHT: J. Barber, Winster, early eighteenth century. A thirty-hour clock with an oak case.

The exact reason for the removal of the original plinth can only be surmised. It may have been deliberately removed in order to fit the clock in under a low ceiling, or it may have rotted badly from years of standing on a damp stone floor. The existing plinth was not attached to the base, just clipped in position, located by four interlocking tongues, almost as though it were designed to be quickly and easily dismantled for moving.

There were several pieces of veneer missing from different parts of the case and a number of quite large splits on both sides of the base. A large scalloped moulding runs across the front and along both sides at the joint between the base and the waist sections. Both joints had come apart, as shown in the photographs.

The waist section was not in bad order apart from the door, which had a large split running almost its full length. There was also a ¼in (6mm) wind in the opening edge of the door between the top and bottom. The hood was in the worst condition of all, being held together with the aid of sticky tape and a few pins. The glass in the hood door was cracked diagonally across from corner to corner and the bottom hinge was missing (probably the cause of the cracked glass). Both front columns and their brass capitals were missing, the

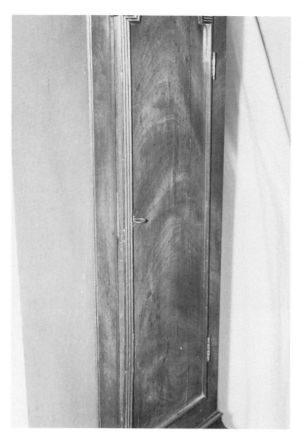

ABOVE RIGHT: Trunk door closed, showing ¼in (6mm) wind on the leading edge.

RIGHT: Joint coming apart between the base and scalloped moulding.

LEFT: Broken wave form moulding on the hood.

BELOW LEFT: Cap missing from reeded finial mounting.

rear quarter columns were there, however, complete with capitals.

Parts of the moulding around the top of the hood had been broken off and were missing. Two of the caps for the reeded finial mountings were also missing. One of the ball and spire finials had become detached from its mounting screw and all three were bent and tarnished.

The three finials, one with a broken mounting screw.

The dial as found; note the crack in the glass of the hood door.

Dial and Hands

The dial was grimy and the numerals and calibration were faded, but otherwise it was quite sound. No maker's name, or town, could be seen on the dial at this time. There is the usual subsidiary seconds dial and calendar aperture with date wheel behind. The steel hands appear to be original. The minute hand needed straightening

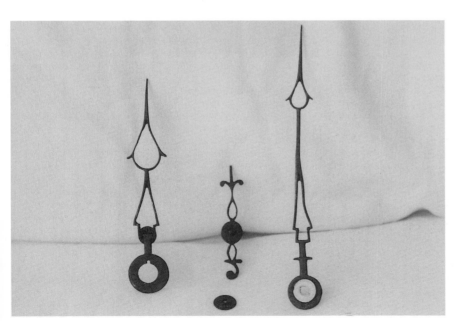

The three steel hands.

but the hour hand had been broken off at some time and a very poor repair made by soft-soldering a patch behind the break to hold both pieces together. The winding key had been made up by soft-soldering the brass shank with the square winding hole to the steel cranked handle. The brass shank was so short that the handle would not clear the hands for winding, which probably accounts for the broken hour hand.

Movement

The movement was complete and apart from an obvious repair to both the rack tail and the hammer arm, and gut lines that were so rotted they would not have supported the driving weights, all was quite sound. Over many years, dust and cobwebs had amalgamated with the oil, which had been liberally applied to every part of the movement, resulting in a sticky black deposit covering everything.

HOW TO FIND PROFESSIONAL HELP AND WHAT IT MIGHT COST

Repair and restoration charges may often surprise people, but it is worth putting the work into perspective and explaining how best to set about engaging the skills of a professional. A professional – as opposed to an amateur – has to charge realistic prices to cover all their overheads. Your clock may not be considered an

The eight-day movement from the back.

The eight-day movement from the left side.

Clock Oiling

It is a common mistake to dip a feather or brush in oil and plaster it all over every part of the movement. This can cause immense damage. Clock oiling is a very important job and over-oiling is in fact worse than under-oiling. Exactly the right amount of the correct grade of oil should be applied to the pivots and the working surface of levers, lifting pins and so on. If too much oil is applied to a pivot hole, the surplus will run down the plate and draw the rest of the oil with it, away from where it is needed. The result is that the clock will soon be running dry, causing premature wear.

Brass wheels working with hardened steel pinions in a clock, where they turn very slowly and the contact surfaces are smooth and polished, require no lubrication. If oil is applied to the wheels it will cause any dust particles, which always find their way into everything, to stick to the gear teeth.

Whenever friction takes place between two dissimilar materials, any particles of foreign matter that become trapped between the two surfaces will always be pressed into, and become embedded in, the softer of the two materials. This creates an abrasive surface to the softer material and as the two surfaces work together, the harder material is slowly abraded away. The result of this can often be seen in old clocks, where the hardened steel pinions are found to be badly worn at the point where the teeth mesh. The brass wheel teeth, however, will often show little sign of wear.

The eight-day movement from the front.

The strike barrel showing rotted gut line; the going side was as bad.

everyday essential like perhaps your television or washing machine, or may not have cost as much to buy as your car, but this does not mean that it is any quicker to repair or that the labour rate should be any less.

Selecting a Horologist

If you need help with your restoration project the best way to select a competent, reliable horologist is to ask around your own circle of friends and acquaintances. Ask if any of them can recommend anyone with whom they have had personal dealings. Just as important, ask if there is anyone who should be avoided.

Even if you find a qualified horologist in your area, it is still worth checking to see if any of your friends have had dealings with them before you make contact. It is always reassuring to have a personal recommendation from someone you know and trust.

If no one you know can recommend a reliable horologist it may be necessary to look for someone who advertises in a trade or telephone directory. When you find a likely candidate, ask them if the job you want doing falls within their field of expertise. Some specialize in certain types of clock and will not touch anything else. If they are unable to help, ask if they are able to recommend anyone who can.

Discuss with your chosen horologist details of the work you would like done. If they have not been recommended to you, satisfy yourself, as far as you can, that they have the ability to carry out the required work to a good standard. You could ask to see their portfolio, if they have one, or ask to speak to one or more satisfied customers for whom they have carried out similar work in the past. If you decide to give them a try, always ask for a quotation before giving them authorization to proceed with any work.

There is no point in handing your clock over more than a few days before the repairer intends to start work on it. Once on their premises you should expect the work to be executed within a reasonable period of time based on the amount of work required. Also, tell your insurance company that the clock is going away for restoration

---

Professional Qualifications

In the UK the British Horological Institute (BHI) is the recognized body for setting and preserving standards of education and qualification for horology. There are several grades of membership, but only two 'qualified' grades. The first qualified grade is 'Member', with the designatory letters MBHI (formerly known as Craft Member or CMBHI). The other grade is 'Fellow', with the designatory letters FBHI. There is no distinction between clocks and watches in either qualification.

In the USA the American Watchmakers/Clockmakers Institute (AWCI) acts as the regulatory body and its qualifications do distinguish between clocks and watches, the designatory letters being either CMC or CMW ('Certified Master Clockmaker' or 'Watchmaker'). The National Association of Watch and Clock Collectors Inc. (NAWCC) also has membership grades, but their members are not recognized as having professional status, being mainly enthusiasts and collectors.

The BHI maintains a list of qualified horologists for the UK by county and town. In the USA the AWCI offers the same service. In Australia and New Zealand the bodies are the Horological Guild of Australasia and the Jewelers and Watchmakers of New Zealand, respectively (see Further Information).

---

and ask them to hold it covered against 'all risks' whilst it is away. Almost certainly, your insurance company will want to know where the clock is going and be given an idea of how long the restoration job will take.

Some firms are reluctant to give a quotation for clock movement repairs without first stripping the movement. There are sometimes hidden problems which only come to light after a movement has been dismantled. This is a reasonable attitude, but it should not prevent them from giving you an estimated cost so that you can gauge the magnitude of expense involved.

If you accept their estimate and give them the authority to proceed, ask them, following the dismantling of the movement, to agree any extra costs with you before they proceed further. This will give you the opportunity to cancel the job if the final quotation is a lot higher than their initial estimate.

Most firms, quite understandably, will make a charge for dismantling and examining a movement and reassembling it again if you choose not to proceed with the repairs. It would be prudent to establish during your initial discussions what this charge is likely to be. As a guide, for a long-case clock, you should allow a minimum of £45, although £80 is more realistic.

If you are planning to do the restoration work yourself, before you make a start read all the books you can find on clock repairing. These days, there is a lot more published information available than there used to be. It would be as well to practise first on mass-produced clocks which can be bought cheaply at auction.

If you wanted to, you could always enrol on one of the BHI 'repair a clock' seminars. These are practical courses, usually of one week's duration, which are run several times a year. All necessary tools and materials, including advice and tuition from a qualified instructor, are supplied at a very reasonable cost; you just turn up with a broken clock. Alternatively, you could enrol on the BHI correspondence or distance-learning course (overseas pupils are also accepted). In the USA the AWCI and the NAWCC run similar schemes.

Learning to repair clocks to an acceptably high standard is not a skill that can be picked up quickly. It takes years of dedicated study and, much more important, a very great deal of practice. It is far from impossible for anyone, with the right attributes and the necessary determination, to learn to become a horologist, but it will take many years of practice to become proficient at it.

Professional Charges

There are no set charges for clock repair and restoration work. Prices vary from being very competitive on the one hand, to very expensive on the other. Geographical location makes a big difference, the highest charges, generally, being in London and other affluent areas, and the lowest being in less affluent and rural areas. The horologist's reputation and clientele make the biggest difference of all. Some of the well-known exclusive city establishments, which cater for the rich and famous, charge extortionate sums for restoration work.

Hourly labour rates vary enormously. At the lower end of the scale, for a one-person business working from home in a rural area, you may find labour rates as low as £16 per hour. Home workers in prosperous town and city locations are more likely to charge between £25 to £35 per hour, depending on skill and reputation. Hourly rate taken on its own can be very misleading as it takes no account of the horologist's skill or workshop facilities. It is best to ask for a quote for the total cost of the job, from someone who can substantiate their ability to do a good job.

Beware of the Well-Meaning Enthusiast

There are many skilled amateurs who are qualified horologists with well-equipped workshops and they do a superb job. However, there are many others who lack the necessary specialist knowledge, practical experience and workshop facilities. Many accomplished engineers have found to their chagrin that clock-making and repairing is not as straightforward as they had at first thought.

Many mechanically minded enthusiasts make the mistake of thinking of a clock movement as nothing more than a gearbox and set about making or repairing a clock with this in mind. They apply the usually accepted engineering tolerances and surface finishes to the various components. A clock movement in fact works in reverse to most ordinary gearboxes. In a longcase clock the great wheel, at power input, completes only one revolution in twelve hours. This is then geared up, through the movement, so that the escape wheel makes 720 turns in the same period of time. Because there is relatively little power or turning moment to start with, by the time the escape wheel is reached the power is minuscule.

Due to the small amount of power available and the extremely high gear ratios involved, unless every aspect of the movement is exactly right the clock is unlikely to work reliably for long periods of time. An experienced horologist will be well aware of the problems involved and know exactly what needs to be done in order to minimize friction and ensure smooth running.

Home Visits and Call-Out Charges

Nobody likes paying call-out charges, but it is perfectly reasonable for any workman to expect to be paid for the time they spend on your behalf. If you ask for them to call on you at home to look at a clock, or anything else for that matter, from the moment they walk out of their workshop you are taking them away from their means of earning money.

A fairly average, local call-out charge (ten-mile radius), across a range of different trades (TV repair, domestic appliance servicing and so on) seems to be about £50 per visit plus VAT. This is for small, independent family firms. Some of the big organizations charge a lot more than this. If you live outside the ten-mile radius, the charge would be higher and most firms appear to charge this extra distance at a mileage rate of something like £1.50 per mile plus VAT.

Any time spent carrying out adjustments or repairs whilst at your home, after the first fifteen minutes from the time of arrival, is charged extra. The usual method used for calculating this is to divide the hourly rate into four and charge this for every extra quarter hour, or part thereof, that is spent at your home. It would not be unreasonable for your horologist to calculate his charges on a similar basis.

CLOCK CASE RESTORATION

Cases for longcase clocks are comparatively large and transport is therefore a big consideration. If you are expecting a restorer to collect the case from your home and deliver it back to you after restoration, you must expect to pay for this service. Sometimes the transport cost is rolled into the restoration cost and not quoted separately; it would be as well to confirm this point at the outset.

For plain oak or mahogany cases in fairly sound condition but requiring a few minor repairs, cleaning off built-up grime and re-waxing, expect to pay a minimum of £150 up to perhaps £275. If the finish is perished or damaged and French polishing is required, it could double the price. If some joints have to be dismantled and re-glued this will add further cost. A case of this type, in very poor condition, is likely to cost over £500 for a professional restoration to a good standard, plus transport.

Pine cases would cost significantly less to restore as they were never built to a high standard from new and the finish applied to them these days is usually only wax. Very often, these cases are seen where pieces of wood have been let in to repair a damaged area. The repaired area is then stained, to give as near a colour match as possible, and then just waxed over, which is accepted practice. As a guide, you could certainly expect to halve the costs quoted above.

Chinese-lacquered cases require very specialized restoration and there are few people who can undertake this class of work. If you have one of these cases and it is in need of restoration be prepared to pay a very high price. You must also be prepared to travel a considerable distance to find a restorer capable of doing a good job.

DIAL RESTORATION

Sometimes a painted dial will only require light cleaning and minor repairs or touching up, the cost for which is likely to be quite a bit less than £150 if carried out at the same time as repairing the movement. If re-calibration is required (repainting numerals and minute track) in addition to the above work, the cost is likely to be around £100 or so. If extensive restoration work is needed, particularly to painted scenes and moon wheels, if fitted, the cost could exceed £200.

Brass dials and silvered dials, provided they are not damaged, are usually less expensive to restore fully. The cost of light cleaning and minor repairs to this type of dial, however, is likely to be the same as stated above for painted dials. If a dial restoration is carried out at some time other than during a movement overhaul, an allowance will have to be made for removing and refitting the hands and dial to the movement. There is also likely to be a call-out charge involved if you want the clock movement collected and returned to your home.

MOVEMENT RESTORATION

The general condition of clock movements can vary enormously. If you are lucky, cleaning and a few minor repairs and adjustments may be all that is required. If so, for thirty-hour longcase movements allow approximately £300 for this amount of work. If most of the pivot holes need bushing and the pivots require attention, or possibly re-pivoting, and perhaps the pallets also need repair, this could double the cost.

On very old clocks the pinions may be badly worn. In extreme cases the wear can be sufficient to prevent the clock from working properly. Sometimes, the meshing wheel can be moved so that it works on an unworn part of the pinion. More than likely, however, a new pinion will have to be made. The additional cost for making and fitting new pinions is indicated below. Broken wheel teeth can often be replaced, but sometimes a wheel may so badly damaged or the teeth so worn that a new one is the only viable answer. Again, an idea of cost for making and fitting new wheels is indicated below.

Antique eight-day longcase movements, requiring the same amount of work as discussed above, will cost approximately 30 per cent more than indicated for thirty-hour movements. Reproduction eight-day weight-driven chiming movements usually only require bushing and cleaning and perhaps a few minor repairs and adjustments. The cost for repairing these clock movements is usually very similar to the thirty-hour movements discussed above.

Extra Costs for Wheel and Pinion Cutting

The following guide prices are for the making and finishing of the new components, ready for fitting only. They do not reflect any labour costs for removing the original components from the movement or final assembly of the new parts to the movement.

Wheels (cut pierced and mounted ready for assembly)	Guide price (each)
Going and strike great wheels	£150
Going and strike train wheels	£85
Escape wheels	£95
Hoop wheel (count wheel strike)	£110
Pin wheels (striking)	£110

Pinions (finished with wheel mounted ready for assembly)	
Pinions with extended arbors (centre, gathering, escape)	£150
Pinion (with wheel mounted on pinion)	£110
Pinion (with wheel mounted on collet)	£130

7 RESTORATION OF THE CLOCK CASE, DIAL AND HANDS

CLOCK CASE

Unless you possess the necessary skills to undertake the restoration work on your clock case you will need to find a competent antique furniture restorer to do the job for you. Just as when choosing a horologist, it is best to ask around your circle of friends for a recommendation. If your clock

---

Conservation or Restoration?

Conservation
There is much concern today over the issue of conservation and the BHI has published a book dealing specifically with the conservation of horological artifacts. In a nutshell, conservationists feel that signs of honest wear and tear in any antique are all part of its history and not only is it acceptable but it is desirable, where possible, to leave things unrestored.

The general consensus of opinion is that every time a clock movement is dismantled and cleaned, microscopic amounts are worn away from all the metal surfaces. This is particularly the case where abrasive paper, or even metal polish, are used. Some chemicals, especially ammonia, used in proprietary cleaning fluids have a long-term detrimental effect on brass, which can lead to 'stress corrosion cracking'.

Conservationists also believe that antique clocks should not be run continuously. They feel that, if run at all, it should only be for demonstration purposes on occasional days through the year in order to preserve them for future generations to enjoy. This policy has currently been adopted by many museums throughout the world.

Conservationists also hold the view that if any work is carried out on an antique clock it is essential to cause as little disturbance to the surrounding mechanism as possible. Any original remnants of material or parts left following a repair should be bagged and labelled and put with the clock. These should be accompanied by a work sheet giving full details of the work done, the name of the horologist and the date.

Restoration
As with all things, there are always varying degrees of compliance. The pure restoration line of thought is diametrically opposed to that of the conservationist. Some restorers believe that a clock should be restored to as near its original condition as possible. They would also advocate that if a part is worn badly enough to impair the performance of a clock it should be replaced. The new part, of course, should be clearly marked with the date confirming its later provenance. They also believe that, once fully restored, it is perfectly acceptable to run an antique clock continuously.

Perhaps it would be better to consider a position between these two extremes, that of 'sympathetic restoration'. Anything in need of repair is attended to using new parts if necessary, to achieve a sound, lasting repair. All new parts should be made and finished in the same style as the original parts. Any existing or original parts which work properly, even if they look a bit jaded, should be retained. Cleaning is fine, but the use of abrasives and polishing should be kept to the absolute minimum.

It is important to be aware of these issues and to bear in mind that just about everything, if it survives long enough, will become an antique in its own right one day. There is no legislation on these matters at present, only guidelines. Probably the best advice is that we should listen to the arguments concerning conservation versus restoration and act responsibly.

happens to be a very valuable piece, you would be well advised to seek the services of a specialist clock case restorer; however, for the majority of clock cases a competent antique furniture restorer should be capable of doing a good job.

The case is the largest and most prominent part of the clock and the first thing people will see when you show them your clock. Therefore, if it is worth restoring at all, it is worth doing properly. Trying to save money by going to someone, just because they are cheap, is not to be recommended. Inappropriate restoration techniques may ruin the antique patina of the case and once the damage has been done the case may be spoilt. A nice wooden clock case is a thing of beauty and, once properly restored, will give many years of pleasure. The advantage of having the job done properly is that the clock will almost certainly appreciate in value.

For the project clock, the chosen restorer collected the clock case and took it back to his workshop to carry out the necessary work. In this particular instance it was requested that he should wait for photographs to be taken after completing each of the four main stages of the work: dismantling, repair, reassembly and applying the finish.

ABOVE: Case with plinth, trunk door and hood removed.

RIGHT: Hood being dismantled.

DISMANTLING THE CASE

The first job was to remove the hood and carefully dismantle it into its many component parts so as to clean up and remake all the loose and broken joints. The trunk door was taken off for repair. The reeded moulding around the edge of the door was removed in order to get a good bearing surface at the sides for case cramps. Cramping was necessary to close up the split which ran from the top of the door to the bottom. In places, the split was a good ⅛in (3mm) wide. It was also necessary to twist the door to get it back to being flat. The main trunk and base section of the case were treated next. The large scalloped mouldings which had become loose around the top and bottom of the trunk were removed so that the joints could be cleaned up ready for re-gluing.

Repair
Hood

The main framework of the hood was reassembled and cramped-up. A few days later, after the glue had dried, several other areas requiring repair were attended to. The original arched top was secured in position; there was a small repair required where a piece of the top had been broken away and lost at some time in the past.

Areas of loose veneer were lifted and re-glued, new pieces were cut and let-in where the original veneer had broken away and become lost. Missing mouldings were replaced with new pieces, made from old wood, to match existing patterns. As the photographs show, new pieces of veneer and small mouldings are held in place, after gluing, with masking tape. This is a much more precise and convenient method for holding small

Another view of the dismantled hood from above.

The hood base, top and left side.

Top right-hand hood joint.

pieces in place than using cramps. After the glue has dried the tape will peel away without damaging existing polished surfaces.

Door hinge blanks, for the hood door, and the brass capitals for the front columns were purchased from one of the clock material dealers. A new piece of glass for the door was obtained from a local source. Ideally, old glass, with bubbles and other imperfections, would be best if a piece could be found big enough for the job in hand. All of the old putty had to be cleaned out of the rebate in the door frame ready for the new glass to be fitted.

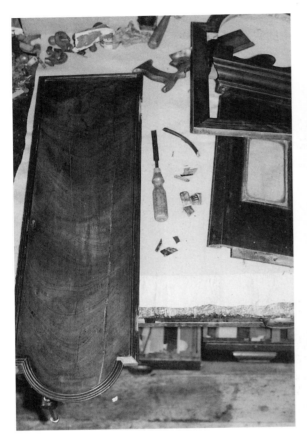

ABOVE LEFT: Trunk door removed, awaiting repair.

ABOVE RIGHT: New glazing beads and two new caps for the reeded finial mountings.

LEFT: Main hood frame reassembled.

New glazing beads for both side windows were cut ready for fitting, together with new caps for two of the reeded finial mounts. Two new front columns were made and proportioned to suit the hood. These were all made from old pieces of mahogany of the same age as the rest of the case and with a matching grain and colour. A repair was also made to the wave-style moulding at the top right-hand side of the hood to replace a missing section.

Old piece of mahogany being shaped for one of the front columns.

New piece of moulding fitted in place.

Door

The large split in the door could have been filled with slithers of matching wood and stained back to get a near match, but even this would have shown up as an obvious repair. Instead, it was decided to cut the top of the door (the cross brace) to release the pressure. The split was then cleaned out and glue applied to the affected area. Three heavy-duty case clamps were used, with suitable protective wood strips, to squeeze the door and close up the split. The whole thing was then twisted slightly, the opposite way to the door's natural distortion, in the hope that when

the glue had dried and the cramps were removed it would end up flat.

After gluing, cramping and flattening the door, long, deep holes were drilled in from the edge to take wood screws which, with the assistance of the glue, should help to prevent the split from opening up again. The screw holes were counter-drilled for about ½in (12mm) in depth to hide the heads of the screws. After fitting the screws the holes were plugged with wood to finish the job. When the glue had cured and the clamps had been removed, the reeded moulding was refitted around the edge of the door.

Repairs to the trunk door, with two cramps left in position.

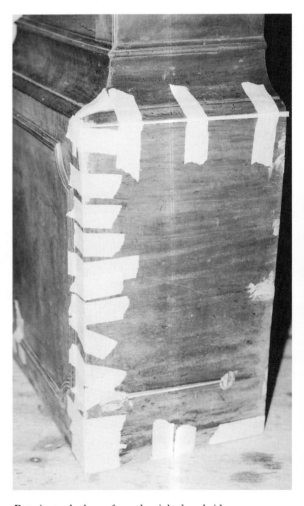

Repairs to the base, from the right-hand side.

Repairs to areas of missing veneer on the base.

Repairs to left side of the base.

Trunk and Base Sections

The joint surfaces for the large scalloped mouldings, around the top and bottom of the trunk, were cleaned off and re-glued into position. Several areas of missing veneer were replaced and loose pieces were re-glued. The backboard was split from the top down to just below the level of the top of the trunk door. This was braced across on the inside, with a piece of old pine batten, to strengthen it and make a sound repair.

The plinth was quite sound in construction, but it was decided, as this plinth was not the original one for the case, to improve the profile of the cut-out for the bracket feet. The profile chosen was typical for the period and probably very closely resembles the one which would have been originally fitted.

Assembly

It was decided to comply with convention and fix the plinth permanently to the base of the clock. Unfortunately, because the replacement plinth had only been made wide enough for the clock to stand on, it was not wide enough to fit around the base in the usual way. Therefore, the border between the top of the plinth and the lower panel moulding is still slightly wider than it should be. The only other option would have been to make a completely new plinth, but as the existing one is probably late Victorian, antique in its own right, it is part of the history of the clock and was, therefore, retained.

The trunk door was refitted and with a little adjustment to the hinges the slight remaining twist in the door was completely disguised. The original lock was repaired and now works perfectly. The new glass was fitted to the hood door and both side panes were refitted using the new glazing beads. Both front columns, complete with brass capitals, were fixed in place and the hood door was fitted on using the new swan-neck hinges. The complete hood assembly was then slid into position at the top of the clock.

ABOVE LEFT: Backboard repaired with piece of old pine batten.

LEFT: Plinth with improved profile to the front cut-out.

Plinth secured in position to the base.

Base from the left.

Base from the right.

Trunk door refitted.

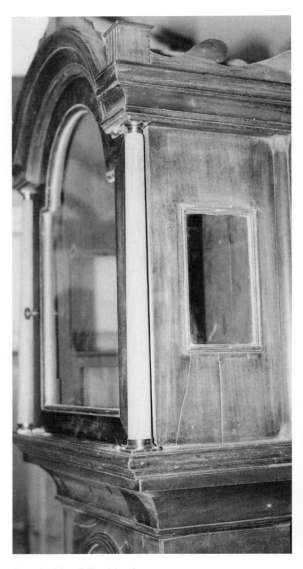

Repaired hood fitted in place.

In keeping with tradition, a long hook is situated in the inside bottom frame of the hood door, close to the opening edge. When the door is closed the hook projects through a hole in the lower part of the hood frame and into the interior of the clock case. A wooden toggle catch is pivoted on the inside of the clock case at this point.

Once the hood is in position, and the hood door is closed, the toggle catch is turned by putting a hand in through the trunk door and reaching up. When the toggle is locked in position, behind the hook, it is not possible to open the hood door or, indeed, to remove the hood

unless the toggle is once more turned to the open position. This ensures that only the person who holds the key to the trunk door is able to make any adjustments to the clock.

Any minor cracks and holes that were too fine to be filled with wood were filled with old, hard beeswax, hand-coloured to match. Old dents and bruises in the wood were left as part of the

Front view of repaired, fully assembled case.

character of the case – these should not be sanded out. All new material, wood and wax filler, were carefully sanded back flush with the original wood surface.

Applying the Finish

The case was lightly stained to bring out the natural beauty of the woodgrain. French polish was

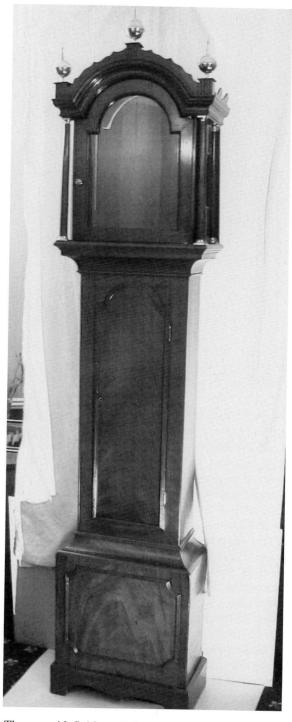

The case with finish applied.

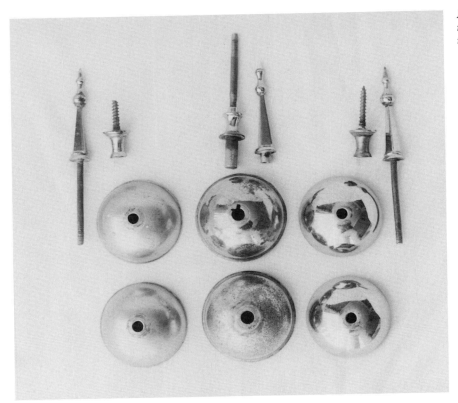

Ball and spire finials repaired and dismantled ready for polishing.

applied next, then rubbed down, and two coats of fine brown beeswax polish were applied. The case should be polished, with the same type of polish, every three months or so to prevent it from drying out, particularly from the effects of central heating.

The ball and spire finials were dismantled and the one with the broken base was repaired. Each piece was then cleaned and polished individually. It is much easier and makes a far better job doing it this way. After polishing, each piece was lacquered to preserve the high lustre. Some people, however, do not like the appearance of lacquered brass, but if the natural polished brass finish is preferred it will need polishing regularly to maintain its lustre. The finials were then reassembled and mounted in their rightful place on top of the hood. The restoration of the whole clock case took forty-two hours, plus three hours for the restoration of the ball and spire finials.

DIAL RESTORATION

The dial of any clock is the second largest area in full view and the eye is automatically drawn to it. No matter how good the case looks, if the dial is shabby it will spoil the whole effect.

Unless a dial restorer has been recommended to you, the only option is to select one from advertisements in horological magazines or from the BHI professional register. Experienced dial restorers will always have a portfolio of their work to show you. They may even have one or more actual restored dials on the premises that you could look at. If they are unable to show you any examples of their work, think twice about using them. A bad dial restoration is far worse than a distressed original dial and should be avoided at all costs.

The dial for this clock is pretty and in basically sound condition. It has suffered from the usual problems associated with old dials – fading badly with age and areas of calibration worn away and

Faded break-arch decoration.

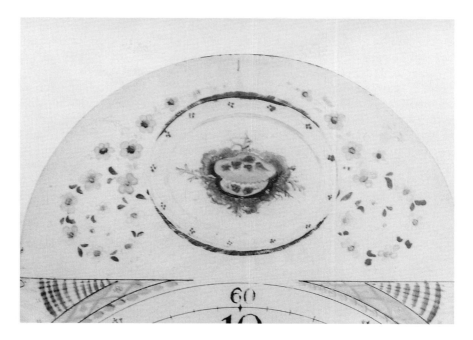

poor touching-in of the Arabic numerals. Fortunately the off-white ground is remarkably good, appearing to be absolutely original with its lightly crazed surface and slight rusting around the edges. It should prove to be a textbook restoration job.

Before work could be started, the cast-iron false plate was removed from the back of the dial; this will only need cleaning up with white spirit followed by wax polishing. This particular false plate has only three feet for attaching it to the

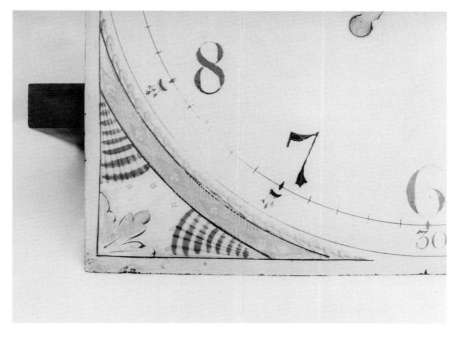

Faded spandrel decoration and calibration.

movement front plate. The feet are brass and will be cleaned up at the same time as the rest of the plate. The back of the false plate bears the name 'Walker & Hughes', Birmingham. As far as is known, Walker & Hughes were in business from about 1811 to 1835, so this information will help in the final dating of the clock.

The date wheel was removed next. This was also in sound condition, with no flaking paint and good, clear calibration, but it was very grubby, the front painted surface looking slightly brown instead of off-white. A brass pipe is riveted to the centre of the date wheel, which was cleaned up and the grime was cleaned off the back of the wheel.

Before any work is done to the dial a colour photocopy can be taken, actual size. This will ensure an accurate record is to hand recording every detail of the existing dial, particularly shape, size, position and colour of all the various features including lines and calibrations. Most towns now have a print shop with colour copying facilities large enough to handle a longcase clock dial. It is important to make an accurate record before cleaning dials or date rings because most of the black lettering and calibration will be lost during the cleaning process.

Before starting on the face of the dial the back surface and dial feet have to be cleaned with cotton wool soaked in white spirit, and then polished

---

Date Wheels

The date wheel pipe fits over a steel post which is riveted on to the back face of the dial. When assembled, a shoulder on the post prevents the front calibrated surface of the date wheel from coming into contact with, and rubbing, the back face of the dial. The outer end of the post has the usual cross hole to take a pin, which prevents the date wheel from coming off while allowing it to rotate freely.

Although the date wheel must be free to rotate, it must also be indexed accurately to indicate the correct date when viewed through the aperture in the dial. If there were no indexing, the wheel might not stop in quite the right place after being moved forward each day by the clock movement. There are several ways of achieving this, but the usual way is to use what is known in horology as a 'jumper'.

A jumper is a long arm with an obtuse 'V'-shaped projection below its outer end. The arm is spring-loaded so as to keep the point of the 'V' located between two teeth on the date wheel, holding it accurately in position. At the appropriate time, a pin fitted to the movement engages a tooth on the date wheel and turns it a little to change the date. As it is turned, one of the teeth on the wheel will push the jumper aside, against the spring pressure, until a position is reached where the point of the 'V' is resting on the point of a tooth. As soon as the wheel is turned a little further and the point of the tooth moves past the point of the 'V', the spring will cause the jumper to snap down between the next two teeth. This action will cause the wheel to jump forward to display the date for the next day.

Sometimes a jumper takes the form of a pivoted arm with a separate spring, but usually it is a long leaf spring with a 'V'-shaped end on it. The jumper fitted to the dial of the project clock is the latter type, made in brass. The foot of the spring is riveted to the bottom edge of the false plate and can be seen in the photograph opposite.

If you study the photograph of the date wheel (opposite), you will notice that it is calibrated with thirty-one days, but it has sixty-two teeth, two teeth for each day. This is because the wheel is moved on, or gathered, by a pin fitted to the hour wheel. The hour wheel, of course, makes two revolutions in every twenty-four-hour period, hence the requirement for two teeth per day.

It is usual to assemble the clock so that the date changing takes place during the small hours. The date change, in the morning, should be set to show the new date accurately lined up with the pointer in the viewing aperture. During the early hours of the afternoon, when the second movement of the wheel takes place, the pointer will lie halfway between the current day's date and that of the following day.

Some clocks have a more sophisticated system incorporating two extra gear wheels to bring about one single date wheel movement per day. The smaller of these two gears is fitted to the front of the hour wheel. This meshes with a larger wheel, giving a 2:1 reduction, fitted on a post attached to the movement front plate. The larger wheel, which turns once in twenty-four hours, carries the pin which engages the teeth on the date wheel. With this system the date wheel is provided with only thirty-one teeth.

False plate, prior to removal. The date jumper is seen riveted to the bottom of the plate.

Front view of the date wheel showing calibration prior to restoration.

Date wheel prior to removal from the dial.

dry. This will prevent old oil, grease and dirt from transferring to the dial's front surface during and after restoration. The brass collets should not be removed from the winding holes as the fixing tabs are usually in a fragile condition and bending them is likely to result in some of them breaking off. They should be polished in situ.

The face of the dial and date wheel need to be cleaned to remove all traces of dirt and grease. Metal polish is used, gently rubbing in a circular motion, a small area at a time. Areas of the original numerals and lines which have been badly over-painted were concentrated on (an original, untouched dial is rare and should be treated with great respect).

The corner spandrels and arch decoration should be treated even more gently when polishing, removing just the dirt and film covering the original colour work. It is imperative that all original colour pigment is retained, intact. The dial surface is now washed clean of any polishing agents with cotton wool soaked in white spirit, and then polished dry with a soft clean cloth. When the surface is clean, any chips or deep scratches are carefully touched in with enamel

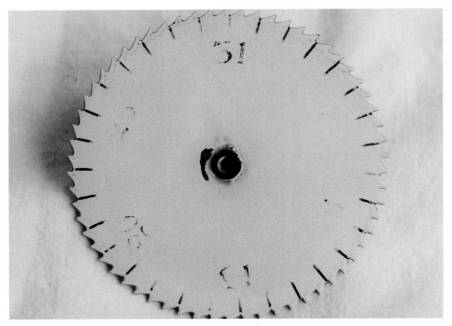

ABOVE LEFT: Dial after cleaning with metal polish.

LEFT: Date wheel after cleaning with metal polish.

paint which has been mixed to the correct shade to match the background.

During the cleaning process most of the calibration was lost, but a ghost image remains of the numerals. A circle of black prick marks, marking the position of the minutes (previously hidden by the calibration) is clearly visible in the photograph right. These prick marks, although fine, are quite deep in the surface of the background and were used as an aid to calibrating the dial when it was originally manufactured.

When the polished dial is held against the light, all the original black markings can be seen as raised bumps. On this dial the maker's name was discernible by this method and an ultraviolet lamp was not required. It is at this stage that these markings can be carefully drawn in with pencil.

Having cleaned the dial and date wheel, and touched in the background, the process of rebuilding the dial can begin. The first job is to apply all the black features: minute and hour markings, numerals, signatures and lines and dates on the date wheel. Dial painters had a line and lettering style of their own, developed over the centuries.

The styles of dial signatures, with their layout and flourishes, are not found in books dealing with calligraphy. The styles used for Arabic numerals is another thing peculiar to dial painting. The layout of Roman numerals is also interesting. In Roman dials the numeral four is almost always set out as 'IIII' instead of the conventional way, 'IV'. The reason is to improve the symmetry of the dial. If it were not for this the numeral 'VIII' on the left side of the dial would make that side look heavy and unbalanced.

Line thickness or 'line weight' can have a dramatic impact on the appearance of a clock dial. The thickness of line used can vary for different features of the dial and knowing where to make a change in line thickness is all part of the dial painter's art. A small increase in line thickness will make the whole dial look much bolder. Later painted dials, with thick lines and bold numerals, look very heavy and overbearing, lacking the finesse of earlier dials.

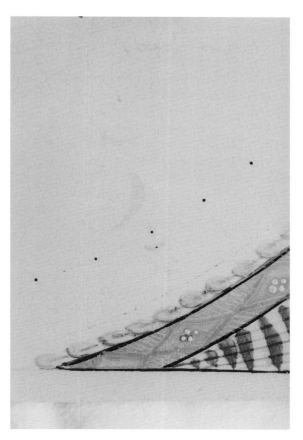

Dial prick marks and ghost image of the number five.

Straight lines are drawn with the aid of a straight edge and the paint is applied with a draughtsman's ruling pen. All curved lines are drawn with a large spring bow compass, the point of which is supported in a piece of thick card taped to the back of the central hand arbor hole. All numerals and the diamond-shaped hour markers are first marked out, in outline, with a

Dates	
Arabic numerals were in normal use between	1800–1820
Walker & Hughes dial-making partnership	1811–1835
Clockmaker Samuel Gill of Rye	1809–1817

fine pen. The dial is then put aside for the outline to dry before finally filling in with a brush.

The next day, when the paint has dried enough for the dial to be handled, the decorations in the spandrels and arch are touched in to restore the colour. It is surprising how faded and washed out the colours become after 200 years. The black calibration and lines give crispness and precision to the dial, but the restored colours soften the appearance and bring the dial back to life.

The finishing touch is achieved by applying gold leaf to certain areas of the dial. Traditionally, gold leaf was applied to the edges of the date aperture, the spandrel borders, and a splash of gold somewhere in the arch decoration. At this stage the dial really looks delightful, but when it is fitted back into the clock case, with the hands in place, it will look stunning.

The complete dial restoration was spread over a two-week period to allow for paint to dry and harden off between each operation. The time spent actually working on the dial, from start to finish, including the date wheel, was thirty hours.

ABOVE LEFT: Dial with all black features finished except for the number ten.

LEFT: Close-up of the number ten showing how the outline for numerals is put in first.

The restored dial.

HAND RESTORATION

The minute and hour hands of the project clock are steel, pierced out of sheet material by hand. They are a little unusual in style, quite delicate, and certainly antique in origin. There is no reason to believe that they are not the original hands fitted to the clock. The minute hand needed straightening and the removal was required of what remained of the old black paint and a little surface rust to prepare the surface for re-finishing. The same treatment was applied to the second hand and, eventually, the hour hand. Before the hour hand could be prepared for refinishing it was in need of repair to a previous unsightly repair, which would restore it to the way it would have looked originally.

A brass washer had been soft-soldered behind a break in the hour hand, to hold the two parts together. This had to be removed before a proper repair could be effected. The area around the repair was heated so as to melt the solder and remove the washer. After removing the washer, it was apparent that the hand had broken off at a weak point either side of the thick arm, at the base of the hand. Once separated, each piece of the hand needed to be carefully filed, around the area which had been joined, to remove completely all

---

Bluing Steel Parts

Many steel clock hands were finished by bluing. Other steel parts are sometimes blued, particularly screw heads. The bluing process is quite straightforward for solid items such as screws, but a lot of skill is involved in successfully bluing intricately pierced antique clock hands. The bluing process involves finishing the steel to a good surface finish and then cleaning thoroughly to de-grease the hand. The item is then gently heated until the prepared surface turns dark blue in colour. The colour changes start with pale straw and gradually deepen in colour until brown is reached, first yellow-brown then red-brown; purple follows, then light blue and finally dark blue.

The colour changes are caused by oxides forming on the surface of the heated steel. If there is any trace of grease, even fingermarks, on the object it will not blue with an even shade across the whole surface. Also, to achieve the best results, with a deep, even colour, the surface of the steel should be polished. Many antique clock hands have become badly pitted over the years and will not blue successfully, so painting becomes the only viable alternative.

Individual small parts can be heated directly by passing them in and out of the flame from a spirit lamp or gas blowtorch whilst being held with tweezers or suspended using a piece of wire. If several items need bluing, screws for instance, these would usually be placed on a bluing tray. This consists of a small brass plate with a series of holes in it and an insulated handle to hold it by.

The threaded part of the screws are placed through the holes in the plate, using tweezers, so that the screw heads rest on the top of the plate. The plate is then moved back and forth over the gas flame to ensure even heating and when the screw heads reach the desired shade of blue they are tipped out into a shallow tray of oil to halt the colour change.

The problem with bluing antique clock hands is that the mass of metal varies throughout their length. At the boss the metal is thick and the width of some of the webs is comparatively wide. The thickness gradually reduces towards the tip and there is usually very fine, fancy piercing at the sides and towards the tip. When the hand is heated the thicker parts take longer to heat up, unless very great care is taken, resulting in different shades of blue.

There are a number of ways around this. One traditional method is to lay the hand on the top of a tray of fine brass filings and then heat the tray from below very slowly so that the whole hand heats up at the same rate, ensuring an even colour. Another method is to heat the hand in bluing salts. Bluing salts become liquid at the appropriate bluing temperature (300°C); a clock hand, or anything else for that matter, left in the salts for a short period of time will be heated evenly throughout. Because the hand is submerged in the liquid salts it is protected from the oxygen in the atmosphere and will not start to colour until removed. Once removed from the salts, because the surface temperature of the hand is even throughout, the whole hand will change colour uniformly.

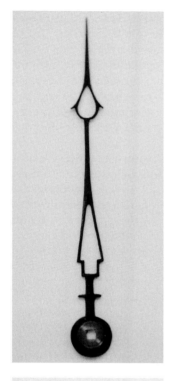

LEFT: The straightened minute hand.

RIGHT: The hour hand after removing the soft-soldered washer.

LEFT: The hour hand following repair.

RIGHT: The three hands finished and painted and the collet polished ready for fitting to the clock.

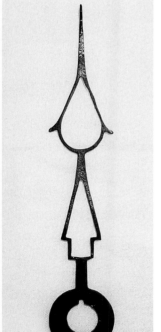

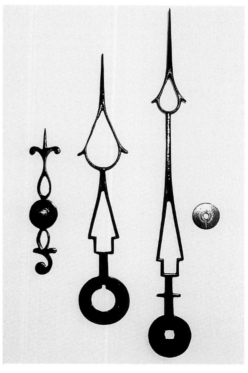

traces of soft solder. The two pieces were to be brazed or silver-soldered together to make a sound repair, with the correct profile.

A small amount of borax powder was mixed with water to form a paste which acts as a flux for the brazing operation. The flux was liberally applied to both joint areas on each piece of the hand, after they had been straightened and flattened. Both pieces were then laid out flat on a fire brick, in the brazing hearth, and arranged in the correct relationship with one another. Tweezers were used to make the final adjustments to their position until the hand looked right.

A fine artist's brush was used to apply more flux to the joint areas without disturbing either of the two pieces. A small piece of hard silver solder wire was cut and laid over each of the joints using tweezers, and more flux was applied using the artist's brush to cover the solder. A propane gas torch with a needle flame was used to make the joint. The area was gently heated to red heat until both pieces of solder melted and flowed into their respective joints. After the hand had cooled down the area around the joints was carefully filed to remove excess solder, leaving the correct profile for the hand. The final operation was to finish the hands with black enamel paint. Painted hands do not look out of place on a painted clock dial. Some clocks, however, particularly high quality clocks dating from an earlier period, have blued hands.

The last job, whilst dealing with the hands, was to restore the brass hand collet. Over the years this had turned black and looked very unsightly. Hand collets, because of their shape and small size, are difficult to hold when trying to polish them. An easy way to polish them is to use a piece of double-sided tape and stick the collet down on to a flat surface. This will hold it quite firm enough for polishing. When finished, a fine knife blade carefully slipped under the edge of the collet will lift it free of the sticky tape. The total time taken to restore the hands and the hand collet was one and a half hours.

8 RESTORATION OF THE CLOCK MOVEMENT

The eight-day movement fitted to the project clock is typical for its period – the dating features would suggest early nineteenth century. There were no obvious signs of serious wear or damage, although the whole movement was so filthy it was difficult to see properly. The movement had not worked for many years and the oil had solidified, sticking everything together like glue.

At a casual glance, two previous repairs stood out because of the way the work had been carried out. The most obvious was the repair to the arm supporting the hammer head. This arm had been broken off at some time in the past and both broken ends had been soft-soldered into a piece of brass tube to join them together again. From a mechanical point of view this was an adequate repair, but it looked very unsightly. The second repair was to the rack tail, which had also been broken off. In this case, however, two pieces of thin brass strip had been riveted across the break, one on either side, to join the two pieces back together. The repair was certainly strong enough, although the work could have been better executed.

The old lines were removed at this stage as they were of no further use. If left in place, they would hamper the pre-cleaning process which was to follow. The easiest way to remove old lines is to use a pair of side cutters and cut them into several pieces, the last piece being clipped off as close as possible to the point where it enters the barrel. The stub end left in the hole is then pushed through from the outside, using a pin punch. The knot will drop into the inside of the barrel, where it can be left. Very often, several knots are found inside a longcase barrel, due to line changes over the years. The hole in the barrel end is usually too small to allow a loose knot to be easily teased out and, as no harm will result, they are traditionally left inside.

The hammer arm, as found.

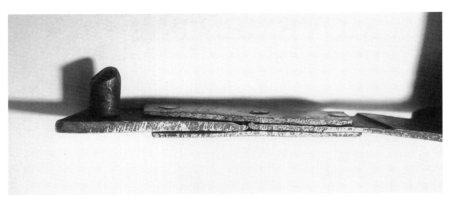

The rack tail repair, as found (seen from below).

Before proceeding further, it was decided to submerge the whole movement, prior to dismantling, in paraffin, leaving it to soak for a few days. Periodically swirling the movement around in the paraffin, and carefully scrubbing as much of the movement as could be reached with an old toothbrush, helped to remove most of the excess grime. The movement was then lifted out of the fluid and left for an hour or so to drip dry. Paper kitchen roll was used to mop most of the liquid off the various movement parts. It was then put aside for a few days to dry further in a warm atmosphere. It is unnecessary to wait for the movement to dry completely. The prime object of pre-cleaning clock movements is twofold; firstly, they are more pleasant to handle and secondly, faults become easier to spot.

It is important to follow a logical sequence when restoring a clock movement. A thorough examination needs to be made of the movement as a whole, prior to dismantling. This is followed by a detailed examination of each and every individual component part during dismantling. Then all remedial work is carried out, and, when finished, a trial assembly is made to ensure everything goes back together and functions properly.

When all repairs and trial assembly are satisfactorily completed, the final cleaning of each individual component can be carried out. There is no point in cleaning the movement prior to carrying out the repairs. Any repair work required will necessitate handling the components and this will cause surface contamination. Finally, the movement is reassembled, lubricated and tested.

A notepad and pen should be at hand from the outset, so that a record can be made of each aspect of the movement requiring attention, and to record all work carried out. Faults usually range from normal wear and tear, to badly repaired or broken components. If it is not noted down at the time, a minor fault can be surprisingly easy to forget. When rediscovered, during assembly, a great deal of inconvenience and wasted time would result.

EXAMINATION FOLLOWING PRE-CLEANING

In addition to the two repairs mentioned above, close examination of the pre-cleaned movement revealed several other faults. A full list of all faults noticed at this stage, together with items requiring more detailed examination after dismantling the movement, are detailed below.

1. Unsightly hammer arm repair.
2. Unsightly repair to rack tail.
3. Gathering pallet held on its arbor using an hour wheel taken from a pocket watch.
4. Gathering pallet tooth repaired with a piece of clock spring and left too thick at tip.
5. Centre wheel bush protruding from movement back plate.
6. Third wheel bush protruding from movement back plate.
7. Escape wheel pinion badly worn.
8. Fly seized solid with its arbor and fly spring not touching arbor.

9. Threaded hole in great wheel (into which the click is screwed) badly worn (strike train).
10. Ditto (going train).
11. Rack spring is a badly made replacement part.
12. Large blob of soft solder holding the crutch to the end of the crutch rod.
13. All screw heads badly chewed at slot.
14. Going train great wheel click, tail missing.

DISMANTLING MOVEMENT AND EXAMINATION OF INDIVIDUAL COMPONENTS

The Back Plate

The back cock and pallets were removed first. The back pallet arbor pivot was worn and so were both pivot holes, one in the back cock and one in the front plate. The working surfaces of both pallets were badly worn, with each showing two distinct sets of wear marks. The bell stand was removed at this stage to leave the back plate clear.

Motion Work and Front Plate

The motion work and other front plate mechanisms were dismantled next. The rack hook and lifting/warning piece were both a good fit on their respective posts. They worked smoothly with no excess shake and showed little sign of wear. The hour wheel/snail assembly was a good fit on the hour bridge pipe; the only fault found was a broken screw in the front of the hour pipe. The screw holds the hour hand securely on to the pipe.

Shake

'Shake' is a horological term used to describe the clearance or freedom of components. If an arbor is taken as an example, axial clearance, between the plates, is termed 'end shake' and clearance between the side of a pivot and the pivot hole is termed 'side shake'.

The rack, apart from the previously discussed repair to its tail, was in good condition and worked properly on its post. The rack spring, although poorly made, could be tidied up and used again. The gathering pallet was a tight fit on

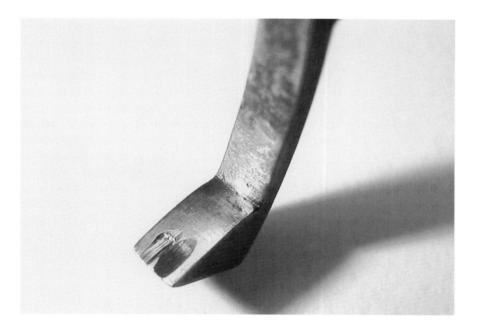

Exit pallet, showing two sets of wear marks.

its arbor and after removal no sign of the usual cross hole, to take a tapered retaining pin, could be found.

The minute wheel on this clock is fitted with a brass pinion and, other than a little wear to the pinion leaves, all was well. The minute post was not fully tightened in the front plate, which is a fault often found. When a clock is working, the direction of rotation of the minute wheel tends to unscrew the minute post. The hour bridge, cannon pinion and minute friction spring were all in good condition. With nothing left attached to the outside, the movement was laid on its back and the pins were removed from the pillars. This allowed the front plate to be lifted off, revealing the wheel trains. Each train would be examined in turn and the findings recorded, starting with the strike train.

Strike Train

The fly was separated from its arbor. The back pivot of the arbor was found to have been re-pivoted (replaced with a new pivot) at some stage in its life. The new pivot was a little small in diameter, showed signs of wear and was also slightly bent. The warning wheel and the gathering wheel,

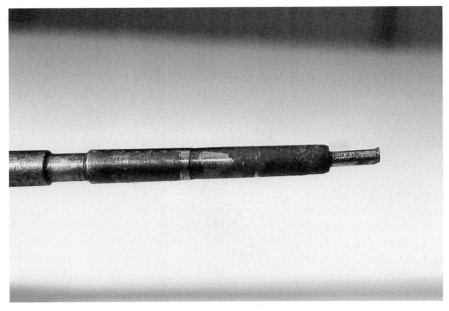

ABOVE: Rub marks on the front of the strike train barrel.

LEFT: Fly arbor rear pivot.

Rub marks on the back of the pin wheel.

together with their respective pivots, were in good condition. The pin wheel pivots were in good condition, but the collet had been moved on its arbor and, although concentric with the arbor, it did not run true in the flat and would need correcting. The photographs (left and above) show the rub marks on the front of the strike train barrel and the back of the pin wheel, caused by the wheel running out of true. There are also signs of fouling between the hammer lifting tail and the front of the pin wheel, at four out of the eight pins.

The barrel and its arbor were sound, although both pivots were scored a little. The great wheel was a good fit on the barrel arbor, but the click was beginning to pull out of the wheel rim due to excessive wear in the threaded hole. This is a serious fault which must be corrected; if the click should pull right out, the weight will crash to the floor. The most likely time for this to occur is on releasing the key, after winding the clock. The pin retaining the key plate was removed and the key plate and great wheel were dismantled from the barrel.

Rub marks around four of the pins on the front of the pin wheel.

The final component to remove on the strike side was the hammer arbor, the back pivot of which was very worn. Most of the pivot holes for the strike train were sufficiently worn to require bushing. In the back plate the following holes needed bushing: fly, gathering wheel, pin wheel, hammer arbor and barrel arbor. The warning wheel pivot hole was the only one in good enough condition to leave untouched. In the front plate the following holes required bushing: warning wheel, gathering wheel, pin wheel and barrel arbor. The fly and hammer arbor pivot holes could be left untouched.

Going Train

The pallet arbor has already been discussed above. The escape wheel and arbor looked fine at first, except for the pinion, which was very badly worn. The back pivot was not only scored but bent as well. There was a second, far less severe, ring of wear in evidence on the pinion, as shown in the photograph. Closer inspection revealed that the back pivot hole had been bushed at some time in the past, with the bush

Click (strike train) pulling out of a worn hole in the strike great wheel.

Escape wheel pinion showing two sets of wear marks.

being left proud on the inside of the back plate. The idea behind this was to move the whole escape wheel and pinion forward slightly, so that an unworn part of the pinion could engage the third wheel, thereby avoiding making a new pinion. This necessitated machining back the shoulder on the front pivot a little way, to allow the arbor to fit between the plates and maintain its end shake. Moving the escape wheel this way would also account for the two sets of wear marks on the pallets as described above.

The third wheel and arbor were sound, except that only the very edge of the pinion was engaging the centre wheel, as shown in the photograph. Closer inspection of the arbor and pinion revealed that the shoulder of the back pivot had been turned back, and another protruding bush had been fitted to the front pivot hole to move the whole arbor back. This was probably an attempt to ensure further that the third wheel engaged an unworn part of the escape pinion; unfortunately this was achieved at the expense of proper engagement between the third pinion and centre wheel.

Escape wheel pivot, slightly bent and scored.

Escape wheel bush standing proud in the back plate.

LEFT: Third wheel pinion barely engaging the centre wheel.

BELOW LEFT: Back centre wheel bush, recessed in the back plate.

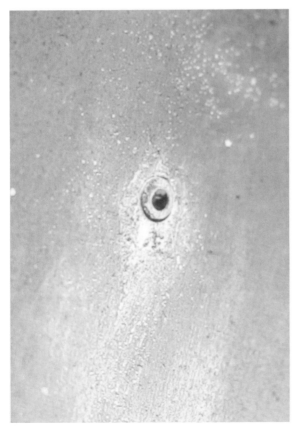

The centre wheel and arbor were in good condition, except for some light scoring to the front pivot and a slight bend to the long extended part of the pivot. The back pivot hole had been bushed, but this time the bush was recessed to allow the centre wheel to move back, presumably to give better engagement with the third pinion. This would have been a successful remedy if a spacer had been fitted between the front pivot shoulder and the front plate to prevent the arbor from working forward and re-occupying its original position. The barrel and its arbor were sound, but both pivots were scored and the click was beginning to pull out of the great wheel rim, just as for the strike side. The great wheel was a good fit on the barrel arbor.

Most of the pivot holes for the going train would require bushing. In the back plate all holes needed bushing: escape wheel, third wheel, centre wheel and barrel arbor. In the front plate the following holes needed bushing: third wheel, centre wheel and barrel arbor. The escape wheel pivot hole could be left untouched.

With the trains dismantled, a thorough check should be made of all wheel teeth and pinion leaves, looking for signs of any bent, cracked or damaged ones. This check will be repeated after final cleaning, prior to reassembly. A slightly bent tooth can cause a clock to stop mysteriously and, very often, they can only be successfully found and straightened with the wheel out of the movement.

It was noticed that a number of parts from this clock showed signs of having been gripped in the jaws of a vice. Standard vice jaws are hardened and have a diamond criss-cross pattern raised on their gripping surfaces. This pattern will emboss itself into the surface of anything held directly in the jaws of the vice. When holding raw materials this is of no consequence, but if finished components are held it is important to protect their surfaces with soft jaws.

Soft jaws are usually made from copper or brass sheet, folded into an 'L' shape, a little longer than the width of the vice jaws. The vice jaws are opened and the soft jaws are inserted with the 'L' inverted, so that one face rests on the top of the existing hard jaw, whilst the other face lies against the criss-cross surface. Any component held in a vice with soft jaws will be gripped between the two smooth brass or copper surfaces and will not be marked. It is important, however, to ensure that all surfaces are free of filings or other foreign matter before tightening the vice, and then only tighten the jaws just sufficiently to hold the component.

REPAIRS

Most of the faults recorded above would require straightforward repair, using traditionally accepted methods. One particular fault, however, would require careful consideration – the badly worn escape wheel pinion. Under normal circumstances any pinion as badly worn as this one would be replaced. It is not generally accepted practice to change the relative working positions of wheels and pinions by arranging bushes in the way described above. In the case of this particular clock, however, someone in the past must have decided to repair it in this way and, judging by the secondary wear, it obviously worked successfully for many years afterwards.

The choices presented were either to re-bush, with all bushes conventionally finished flush with

Train Count

It is usual practice, during a major repair or restoration, to record the train count of a clock (the number of teeth on each wheel and pinion). For the project clock the train count was as follows:

	Wheel	Pinion
Motion Work		
Cannon	n/a	36
Minute	36	6
Hour	72	n/a
Going Train		
Escape	30	7
Third	56	8
Centre	60	8
Great wheel	96	n/a
Strike Train		
Fly	n/a	7
Warning	42	7
Gathering	49	7
Pin	56	8
Great wheel	84	n/a

the inside of the plates, and all wheels and pinions working in their original relative positions. This would require a new escape pinion to be made. The alternative would be to position all new bushes to match the existing ones. The problem of engagement between the centre wheel and the third pinion, discussed above, could be corrected if the front centre wheel pivot hole bush were left slightly proud inside the front plate.

It was decided to adopt the second option for the following reasons. There is probably at least another half-century of wear left in the existing escape pinion with the arbors working as currently positioned. If the existing worn bushes are replaced without further work being done to the plates, the clock would work perfectly well and this would be the best option all round from a conservation point of view. Eventually, the time will come when the escape pinion will have to be replaced. The bushes will also need replacing by then and this would be the ideal time to fit new bushes in the conventional way, restoring the movement to its original layout.

Jacot Drum

Clock Jacot drums are usually supplied as attachments for the lathe. They consist of a drum-shaped billet of hardened steel approximately 1in (25mm) in diameter and ½in (12mm) long. The drum has a number of equally spaced grooves running lengthways on its circumference. Each successive groove is a little wider and deeper than the one before and the bottom of each groove has a radius. The drum is attached to a holder by a spindle running through its centre, which also allows the drum to be rotated to any desired position. The shank of the holder is held in the tail stock of the lathe.

The drum is attached to the holder with its axis in line with the lathe centers, but offset below the lathe centre height by an amount equal to almost half its diameter. The drum can be rotated on its spindle until the appropriate-sized groove is at the top, in line with the lathe centres, where it can be locked in position. The groove width selected should closely match the diameter of the pivot it is intended to support. The purpose of the offset holder is to ensure that each of the grooves, or 'beds' as they are called, will support the pivot at centre height, whilst in the lathe. The pivot should be supported for its full length by the selected bed.

With the worn pivot supported in the appropriate bed, the pivot at the other end of the arbor may be supported in a female centre at the lathe head stock. It is possible to drive the arbor, at slow speed, using the lathe motor. However, a much better and safer method is to attach a split pulley or screw ferrule to the arbor and drive it by hand, using a bow. Bows are easily made from a length of wire coat hanger, bent to a bow shape, and a piece of fine clock line. If the bow has an overall length of about 16in (400mm), this will be adequate. The pivot is prevented from coming out of its bed, in the Jacot drum, by holding a pivot file across the top of the pivot, at right angles to the axis of the arbor.

Jacot drum.

Split pulley fitted to third wheel arbor. Arbor set up in Jacot tool.

Close-up of pivot in Jacot bed, shown after filing and burnishing.

Jacot Drum *continued*

The line on the bow is wrapped once around the pulley, such that it forms a straight line across the top of the pulley. The upper surface of the pivot will then move in the same direction as the bow. As the bow is pulled towards the operator, the pivot file is pushed away. A steady downward pressure is exerted on the file as it is worked to and fro against the rotating pivot. This will remove any roughness and scoring from the pivot whilst the top surface of the Jacot drum will ensure that the file leaves the pivot parallel. The edge of the file should be kept firmly against the shoulder of the pivot at all times to prevent a step or radius from forming at the root. No cutting action takes place when the bow and pivot file move in the reverse direction. If the line is wound on the split pulley the wrong way, the direction of rotation of the pivot is reversed, making work awkward.

When all traces of roughness are removed from the pivot, the arbor is lifted clear of the lathe, and the pivot and its bed in the Jacot drum are thoroughly cleaned. The arbor is then placed back in the lathe and this time the pivot is burnished to a high mirror-like finish. The pivot burnisher is used in the same way as the pivot file. For this operation, the pivot, bed and burnisher should be lubricated with clock oil.

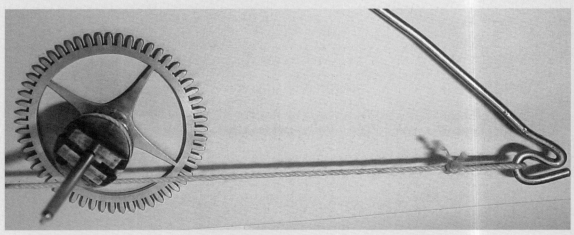

TOP: *Bow and line shown correctly fitted to pulley.*
BOTTOM: *Bow and line shown incorrectly fitted to pulley.*

Back Plate

The rear pallet arbor pivot was restored with a pivot file, and then burnished, whilst being supported in a Jacot drum in the lathe.

Because the crutch rod projects at 90 degrees to the pallet arbor, it prevents full rotation of the pivot in the Jacot drum. Therefore, the arbor must be rotated by hand, as far as it will go in each direction. Despite this, an acceptable job can be achieved if approached with care.

Whilst dealing with the pallet arbor, it would be convenient to attend to the pallets and the escapement generally, before proceeding with either of the trains. However, there is no point in attempting to resurface the pallets and adjust their depth with the escape wheel until all necessary repairs have been carried out to their respective pivots and pivot holes. Any bent or damaged escape wheel teeth should also be attended to, prior to adjustments being made.

At some time in the past, the pallet arbor pivot hole in the back cock had been 'punched-up'. This involves indenting the area around a pivot hole on its worn side, using a round-nosed punch, and has the effect of closing the hole to counteract wear. In the case of a back cock the wear takes place at the bottom of the hole. The practice of punching clock plates causes serious defacement and is a botch to be avoided at all costs. Worn pivot holes should be bushed, using thin-walled bushes, to leave as much of the original material as possible.

The back cock was repaired by bushing, using a bush of appropriate size. The punch marks were left as part of the history. The clock plates were reassembled, followed by the pallet arbor. The back cock was offered up and the bush carefully eased with a broach until a snug fit was achieved with the pivot. A round broach was selected and the hole burnished to a free fit with the pivot. The front pallet arbor pivot hole was then bushed in similar fashion.

The escape wheel back pivot was straightened by holding it in the lathe, using a collet of the correct size. The lathe spindle was then slowly rotated by hand, which caused the pivot at the opposite end of the arbor to describe a small circle. By carefully manipulating the outer end of

Back cock, showing punch marks around the lower part of the pivot hole.

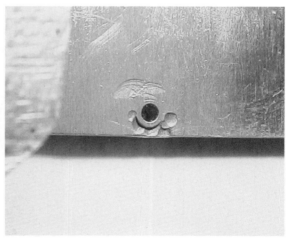

Back cock pivot hole after bushing.

Bushing Clock Plates

The constant driving force between a wheel and its meshing pinion causes the pivots to work against one side only of their pivot holes. As a result of this, the eventual wear produces elongated holes. When they become worn to the extent that they require bushing, it is important first to remove just sufficient metal from the unworn portion of the hole to restore concentricity with the original pivot hole centre. This can be accomplished by careful filing, using a fine round file.

Before filing begins, however, it is advisable to scribe a small witness ring around the worn hole, within the oil sink area, to indicate where metal should be removed. To do this, first assemble the plates with the arbor in place. Push the pivot towards the unworn part of the pivot hole by placing a finger against the side of the arbor. With a sharp scriber, carefully mark a concentric ring around the pivot, just large enough in diameter to enclose the worn part of the hole. The irregular-shaped hole is then filed out to the scribed circle. Sometimes the oil sink can be used as a guide to filing, if it is found to be concentric with the original hole, but, unfortunately, oil sink concentricity cannot be taken for granted.

Once concentricity has been restored, a cutting broach is used to increase the diameter of the hole gradually until it will accept a bush. If an attempt is made to broach an elongated hole without first restoring concentricity, the cutting pressures will force the broach midway along the elongation. This will produce a hole with its centre out of position from the original pivot hole, affecting the depth (meshing) of the wheel and pinion.

Broaches are available in a range of sizes and they resemble spikes with their long, slow taper gradually increasing in thickness towards the handle. Cutting broaches are pentagonal in cross section, providing five full length cutting edges. If a broach is lightly pushed into a hole and rotated, simultaneously, it will progressively open the hole to a greater diameter by virtue of the taper. When using a broach it is important to keep

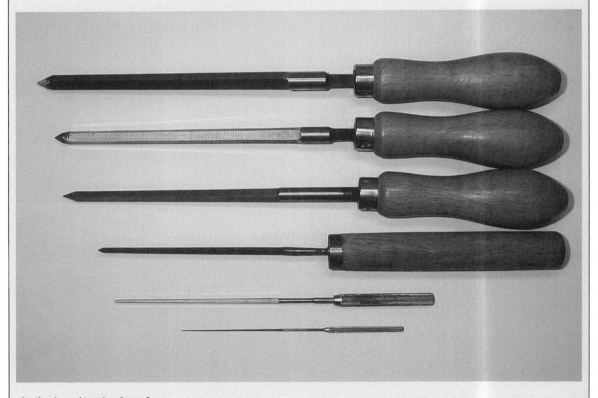

A selection of cutting broaches.

it perpendicular to the clock plate at all times. This will ensure that the bush and therefore the pivot hole in the bush are square with the plate.

Because broaches are tapered, the holes they cut will also be tapered. For this reason, the outside diameter of the bush must have a matching taper if it is to fit the broached hole properly. Holes should be broached, from the inside surface of the plate, until the bush will enter for approximately half the thickness of the plate. It is then driven in tightly, until its end is flush with the inside of the plate. The plate is turned over and supported on a polished bench stake (anvil), the end of the bush, within the oil sink, is then riveted with a round-nosed punch. The spherical radius, within the oil sink, can be finished off with a special oil sink cutting tool. The inside face of the bush, if nicely flush, can be left as it is or, if preferred, finished with progressively finer emery buff sticks until it becomes impossible to detect.

The reason for broaching from the inside surface of the plates is that the taper will ensure the bush is unable to work its way through, if for any reason it should become loose in the plate. The shoulder on the pivot will, of course, prevent it from coming out backwards. The pivot hole in the bush is now broached out until the pivot will just enter. The final smooth finish to the pivot hole and the side shake is achieved using a round broach. Round broaches have no cutting edges at all. They are lubricated with oil and then used in the same way as a cutting broach, which produces a burnished surface to the pivot hole. The pivot hole should be burnished until the pivot is nicely free.

It is best to bush one hole at a time and afterwards, with the arbor fitted between the plates, try the pivot for freedom. The arbor should spin perfectly freely in the normal horizontal position and in the vertical, front plate up and front plate down positions. When finished, all arbors should fall freely, with an audible metallic clunk, when the movement is turned from front plate up to front plate down.

continued overleaf

After bushing a pivot hole, the oil sink is cleaned out with an oil sink cutter.

Bushing Clock Plates *continued*

Clock bushes are commercially available in a range of popular sizes. They are, however, very easy to make with a lathe, allowing the convenience of producing the exact size required to suit the job in hand. Within reason, the wall thickness of a bush should be kept to the minimum and the outside diameter well within the area of the oil sink. The length should be just sufficient to leave a small allowance for light riveting in the oil sink when the inside face is flush with the inside of the plate. If this method is followed, very little work will be required in cleaning up after bushing.

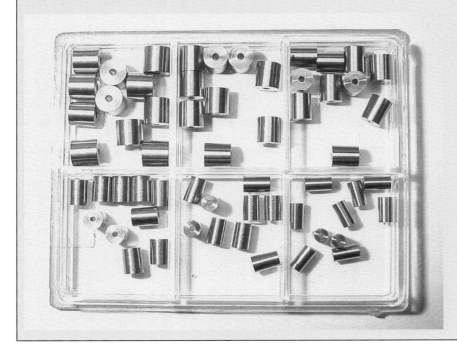

Assortment of commercially available tapered clock bushes.

the arbor, the pivot was straightened. This is a far safer method than attempting to bend a pivot straight with a pair of pliers. Once straightened, the pivot was carefully restored in the Jacot tool.

After checking each escape tooth for straightness, the arbor was set between female centres in the lathe to check the escape wheel for true running. A piece of white paper is taped to the tool rest and its edge gradually brought closer to the tips of the wheel teeth. The wheel is turned one tooth at a time by hand and, using a powerful eye glass, the gap between each tooth tip and the edge of the paper is carefully compared. If there is more than a slight difference between teeth the high ones must be very carefully stoned back with a fine Arkansas stone. Paper is used to avoid

damage to the teeth in the event that one should accidentally touch as the wheel is turned.

The back pivot hole for the escape wheel was bushed and in this case it was possible to open up the old bush and fit the new bush inside it. The plates were again reassembled with just the escape wheel fitted. The new bush was opened with the broach, just sufficiently to give the correct working fit and then burnished. The pallet arbor was fitted in place so that the escapement action could be checked. It was estimated that a piece of 0.010in (0.25mm) thick clock mainspring on each pallet would produce the desired escapement action.

A length of mainspring, of the correct thickness, was taken from stock and two small pieces were cut from it. Each piece was made a little larger in area than the area of the pallets, to make fitting easier. Both pieces of spring were then curved slightly to match the curve of the pallets, and the inside curves of both were roughened with abrasive paper and tinned with soft solder. Both pallets were treated likewise.

After applying flux to the surface, the new facings were held in place on the pallets with a pair of crocodile clips, modified for the purpose. The pallets were heated until the solder melted, the crocodile clips ensuring that the facings were pushed hard against the pallet surfaces. When cool, the clips were removed and the pallets thoroughly washed in white spirit, to remove all traces of flux.

The new facings were then stoned back at the sides to remove the excess mainspring material. A carborundum stone was used to remove most of the excess, and the job was finished with a fine Arkansas stone. The tips of the facings must be stoned back with great care, a little at a time, and then tried in the movement to check the escapement action. If too much material is removed from either pallet tip the escape wheel will be released too early, resulting in excessive drop on to the opposite pallet. When all adjustments have been made, the working surfaces of each pallet must be polished so that friction is reduced to the minimum possible.

Escape wheel set up between centres, checking each individual tooth against a paper edge.

Strike and Going Trains

Except for the barrel arbors and centre arbor, all remaining pivots were treated together. Bent ones were first straightened and those with scored and worn surfaces were restored in the Jacot tool. The barrel arbor pivots, being too big to fit the Jacot tool, were restored using a bigger lathe. The centre wheel was assembled between the plates and its long front arbor extension was carefully straightened by tapping the outer end with a hide hammer. The front centre wheel pivot is in the middle of its very long arbor and was also restored in the bigger lathe.

The back pivot for the hammer arbor, because the hammer arm projects at 90 degrees, was treated as described above for the pallet arbor. The soft-solder repair to the hammer arm was heated

New pallet facing fitted, ready for finishing.

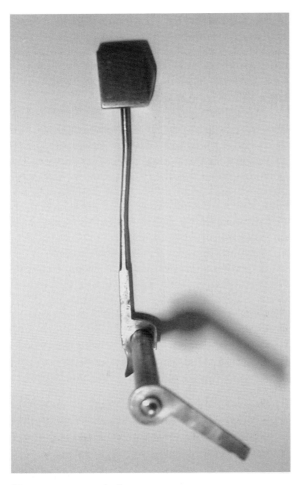

Hammer arm repaired.

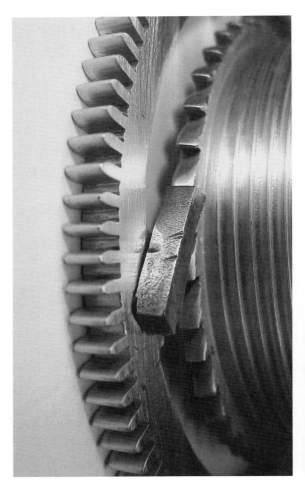

Going click fitted to its repaired hole; note the missing tail when compared to the photograph on page 102.

and dismantled. Both broken ends were cleaned up and arranged on the brazing hearth, fluxed and brazed. The joint was cleaned up with a fine file and abrasive paper. When finished, the repair was difficult to detect. The pin wheel arbor was mounted between centres in the lathe and the collet carefully warmed until the wheel could be set straight. Afterwards, a check was made to ensure that the wheel was still concentric with its arbor.

The threaded holes for the clicks, one in the rim of each great wheel, were in very poor condition. The clicks have an integral thread, projecting at right angles to the middle of one side, and they

screw into the great wheels to engage the ratchet teeth on the barrels. The going click looks different because its tail had been broken off at some point in its life, but because this will have no effect on the working of the clock, nothing was done about it.

There was so little material between the hole in the going great wheel and the root of the wheel teeth, that drilling the hole out to a larger size was considered unsafe. Instead, a short length of threaded brass rod was silver-soldered into the hole, the repaired areas being filed flush afterwards, on both sides of the wheel. A hole was drilled in the original position, chamfered both sides, then

Sprung Rack Tails

Sprung rack tails are a safety feature provided on many clocks. If the front view of the movement is studied, it will be appreciated that at every hour, when the rack drops, the beak will contact one of the twelve steps on the snail. Should the strike train fail to run for any reason, the rack will not be gathered up and the beak will remain in contact with the step on the snail. From one o'clock through to twelve o'clock this would not present a problem, as each successive step is lower than the one before. At each hour, as the rack is released, the beak would drop on to the next lower step.

At twelve o'clock, however, the leading edge of the snail, which separates the twelve o'clock and one o'clock steps, will make contact with the beak on the rack tail. The leading edge of the snail and the tip of the beak are chamfered, and as the leading edge comes round, the mating chamfers will cause the rack tail to flex safely aside. Unless provision is made for the rack tail to flex to the side, under these circumstances either the hands will be prevented from moving or the clock will stop, depending on the strength of the minute friction spring.

Leading edge of the hour snail contacting the rack tail beak causing it to spring aside.

tapped 5BA , to match the thread on the clicks. Both wheels were treated in the same way.

The fly spring was adjusted and its rivet tightened so that it would provide the necessary driving friction between the fly and its arbor. When the strike train runs, the rotating fly provides the required air-braking effect to the train. At the end of a striking sequence, the train locks and all wheels and arbors stop abruptly. Because the fly is revolving at speed, if it were positively attached to the fly arbor when locking occurred, inertia might cause damage to the train. As it is, when the arbor locks, the fly spring slips on the arbor, allowing the fly to slow down without causing harm.

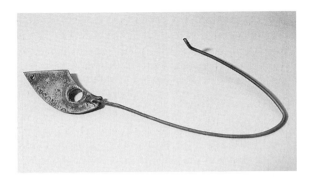

Rack spring, before.

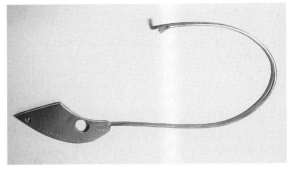

Rack spring, after.

Motion Work and Front Plate Mechanism

The broken screw in the hour pipe was carefully drilled out and the hole subsequently tapped ten BA for a depth of ¼in (6mm); a new steel screw was provided. The piece of spring steel previously used to repair the gathering pallet tooth was stoned off from the back, so as to thin down the leading edge. If the edge is left thick, apart from looking unfinished, there is a danger it could butt on the rack teeth whilst gathering. The previous repair to the rack tail, although not aesthetically pleasing, was robust. There was sufficient sideways resilience at the root of the tail to allow it to spring aside, if the leading edge of the snail should strike the beak. Therefore, it was decided to leave it as part of the clock's history.

The foot for the rack spring had been cut out of the plate of an American clock – most of the name 'Ansonia' could still be seen, engraved on the surface. The brass wire, acting as the spring, had been roughly soldered to the foot. It was decided to retain this component, while improving the quality of the soldered joint and reshaping the wire spring to an improved profile. The purpose of the large blob of soft solder on the crutch was a mystery; once heated and removed, the crutch was found to be securely brazed to the crutch rod.

Every single screw head in the clock was badly chewed at the slot, as a result of using the wrong sized screwdriver in the past. The blade of a screwdriver should fill the slot in a screw for its full width. If any screwdriver blade shows signs of wear it should be attended to before it is used.

Each screw was held by its threaded diameter, in a collet, and run at moderate speed in the lathe. The damaged areas were then carefully dressed up with a fine file, followed by ever finer grades of abrasive paper. Just sufficient material was removed to leave the screw heads tidy. To take out all marks would necessitate removing an excessive amount of material.

TRIAL ASSEMBLY

With all remedial work concluded, each train was assembled and checked separately. Every pivot was checked for side and end shake and all wheels and pinions were checked for depth (engagement). The great wheel was carefully pulled round by hooking a fingernail behind the teeth. Each train was tested for smooth running by this method, for two revolutions of the great wheel, in each of three different positions.

Apart from the normal running position, the movement was tested in the horizontal (arbors running vertically), once with the back plate at the bottom and once with the front plate at the bottom. This was to ensure that the pivots did not bind in their holes when the shoulders were running against the plates. With the movement held in the horizontal position, each arbor should fall freely to the lower plate, after being lifted to touch the upper plate and then released. If there is any tendency to stick, or if there is not a definite metallic clunk as they fall, the cause should be investigated and corrected.

CLEANING

The movement was again dismantled and each individual component was put to soak, for half an hour, in a water-based clock-cleaning solution. It is important to read a manufacturer's health and safety instructions before using any chemicals. It is also vital, from the conservation point of view, that ammoniated cleaning fluids are only used in the diluted state. Follow the manufacturer's instructions and, if anything, use a weaker rather than stronger mixture.

On removal from the cleaning fluid, each part was carefully scrubbed, with an old toothbrush, followed by a hot water rinse, then dried off. Each piece was carefully examined and any dirt or tarnish still adhering was removed using a rubber block, impregnated with abrasive. These blocks are commercially available in three different grades, course, medium and fine, the latter having a very gentle action. Another big advantage with these blocks is that they are very easily cut to a particular profile, using a scalpel. This makes them ideal for getting between pinion leaves, wheel teeth and other awkward places.

After being handled and treated with abrasives, every component is carefully cleaned in a good quality spirit or oil-based cleaner, and then rinsed in the appropriate rinsing solution for the particular cleaning fluid used. This will remove all fingermarks and any remaining traces of dirt or abrasive material. Drying is usually carried out in a stream of warm air in a drying chamber; avoid breathing the fumes.

It is obvious that great care should be taken to avoid any of the cleaned components coming into contact with particles of dust and dirt. It is also particularly important to avoid touching any cleaned component with bare fingers. Cotton gloves or rubber finger protectors (silicone-free) should be worn. Bare fingers will leave traces of perspiration and grease on the surface of the metal. This may go unnoticed at first, but after a short time fingerprints may appear as brown stains on brass components and as rust on steel parts.

Brass components, particularly plates, can be buffed up using a soft or medium grade clock brush and chalk. The chalk is available from the material dealers in refined and purified block form. Ordinary chalk will not do. The bristles of the brush are drawn across the block of chalk, so that they become charged with chalk particles. The brush is then briskly rubbed over the brass, with light to moderate pressure, recharging the bristles regularly. Any marks left by the rinsing fluid as it dried will be removed by this treatment and the brass surface have a slight polish.

The oil sinks (the spherically radiused depression on the outside of each pivot hole) can be buffed by laying the plates on the work bench, oil sink uppermost. A small square of chamois leather is placed over the sink and pushed into it with the end of a piece of stout peg wood. The peg wood should be about ¼in (6mm) in diameter and 8in (200mm) long. The operating end should be sharpened to a blunt chisel shape, and the tip radiused, to match the oil sink. A perfect match is not necessary as the chamois will compress between the two surfaces. The peg wood is gripped between the palms of both hands and simultaneously pushed down into the chamois square and reciprocated, by rubbing the hands back and forth.

Every pivot hole and pipe should be thoroughly pegged out with a piece of sharpened peg wood. The sharpened end should be given a long, gradual taper; it should be kept firmly pushed into the pivot hole, or pipe, and twirled round between the fingers. When withdrawn, the end will be found to have a black ring of dirt impressed into it. The end should be resharpened and the process

---

Chalk Brushing

It may seem contradictory to advocate chalk brushing clock parts and, at the same time, say that they must be kept dust-free. However, if the proper chalk is used, in conjunction with a clean brush, no harm will be done. Clock makers have used this method for centuries. After pegging the pivot holes and blowing down with the bellows, all parts will be left perfectly clean.

repeated, as many times as necessary, until the point comes out as clean as it went in. Each hole should be pegged from both sides. The individual components should now be lightly dusted over with a clean, soft brush, followed by blowing down with a clock maker's bellows, not forgetting to blow air through the holes. With everything thoroughly cleaned, a final close inspection of the wheel teeth is made; if all is well, the movement is ready for reassembly.

ASSEMBLY

The working area of the bench should be covered with several sheets of clean paper before any assembly work begins. This will ensure that cleaned parts do not become contaminated by dirt that may be present on the surface of the bench. Before the trains can be assembled between the plates, the sub-assemblies must first be put together. The clicks and click springs are fitted to their respective great wheels and both great wheels are then fitted to their barrels and retained in position with the key plates. The fly and fly arbor must also be assembled, not forgetting to check the fly spring for tension. These parts should have their working surfaces lubricated during assembly. The lines could also be attached to the barrels at this time, or left until the movement is assembled – this is a matter of personal choice.

It will be found easier to attach the hammer spring to the back plate before assembling the train. The back plate should then be placed on the bench with its back on the clean bench paper. The centre wheel is fitted first, followed

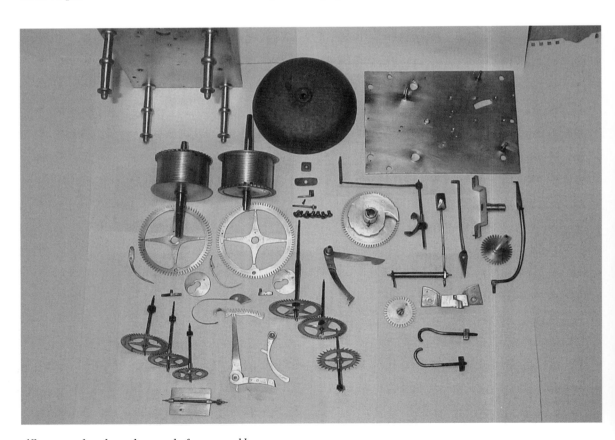

All parts gathered together, ready for reassembly.

by both barrels. The remaining train wheels, fly and the hammer arbor can then be assembled. Unlike the going train, the strike train must have the pin wheel, gathering wheel and warning wheel arranged in the correct relationship with one another for the strike to function properly.

The pin wheel must engage the gathering pinion in such a way that when the hammer lifting tail drops off a pin on the pin wheel, the gathering pallet tail is in position to engage the pin on the rack, thus locking the train. With the train locked, the gathering wheel must engage the warning pinion so that the warning wheel will make not less than one third of a turn, nor more than half a turn, at the run to warning. The importance of setting these three wheels correctly cannot be overemphasized.

With the arbors thus arranged, the front plate should be gently lowered into place. It can sometimes be a tedious job, locating all the pivots correctly, so as to enable the front plate to fall into place. It is important that the front plate is kept flat as it is lowered into place, and that undue force is not used, otherwise there is a real danger that some of the pivots may become bent. Once the front plate is properly home, it should be pinned in place. Before proceeding further, check to ensure that the strike train is set up as just described.

Make sure that both trains run freely by gently pushing the great wheels with a gloved finger. If all is well, oil the front pivots only at this stage. Always use a good quality clock oil and apply just sufficient to be visible in the bottom of the oil sinks. Satisfactory oiling can only be achieved

Movement on test, viewed from the left.

Movement on test, viewed from the right.

using a clock oiler, with a properly formed end, or an automatic oiling device. With the front plate pivots oiled, the motion work and other front plate components should now be fitted. The minute friction spring and cannon are fitted and lubricated, followed by the hour bridge. The posts for the minute wheel and lifting/warning piece should be lubricated, and these components fitted but not pinned in place yet. The minute hand should be held in position, on the squared end of the cannon, and turned to indi-

cate the hour position. With the cannon held in this position, the engagement between the teeth on the cannon pinion and the minute wheel should be positioned so that the lifting pin just releases the lifting piece. The minute hand can now be removed.

The rack post and the pipe on the hour bridge should now be lubricated. The rack and the hour wheel are then placed in position. On some clocks, it may be necessary to fit these two components simultaneously, as the hour wheel lies

Résumé of Restoration Times Taken, Costs, Approximate Value and Dates

Restoration Times Taken

TASK	HOURS
Case restoration	42
Finial and hand restoration	4.5
Dial restoration	30
Movement restoration	40
Setting up the clock and final regulation	1
Total restoration time	**117.5**

Costs

Price paid for clock	£1,335
Cost of case restoration	£715
Cost of dial restoration	£140
Cost of movement restoration	£1,040
Ancillary costs (brass capitals, hinges, etc. plus consumables)	£110
Total cost	**£3,340**

Value of the Restored Clock
- Retail price from a dealer's showroom, complete with at least a twelve-month guarantee, delivered to your home and set up = approx. £6,500
- Probate value (likely auction price) = approx. £4,500
- Insurance value: this should be sufficient to allow for buying a replacement clock, of the same type and style and in the same condition, from a dealer's showroom. Therefore, the insurance value should be set at a minimum of the retail value plus a contingency allowance of 10 per cent or 15 per cent. It is important to monitor value trends and to obtain a professional valuation at least every three years.

Date of Clock
- Arabic numerals were in normal use between 1800–1820
- Walker & Hughes dial-making partnership = 1811–1835
- Clockmaker: Samuel Gill of Rye = 1809–1817
- Clock case = c.1800
- Movement = c.1800

For this particular clock, narrowing down the possible date of manufacture is made very easy. The clockmaker Samuel Gill worked at Rye for only eight years, from 1809 until 1817. Reference: *The Clockmakers of Sussex*, by E J Tyler (1986).

between the rack and its tail. The hour hand is held in position on the hour pipe and, without disturbing the position of the minute wheel, the hour wheel is positioned to indicate twelve o'clock. The hour hand can now be removed. The rack hook post is lubricated and the rack hook fitted; all posts can now be pinned. With the strike train correctly positioned for the locking, the gathering pallet is fitted. On this movement, the gathering pallet is retained by lightly driving it on to its tapered square arbor; for security, a brass ferrule is also fitted. The rack spring is fitted last, not forgetting to lubricate its contact point with the rack.

Stand the movement the right way up, on the clean bench paper, with the back plate facing the front. The bell stand should be fitted next, followed by the pallet arbor and back cock. The pallet arbor pivot holes and all the pivot holes in the back plate should now be oiled with clock oil. The points of contact between all levers and pins on the front plate and the pin wheel and warning wheel pins, between the plates, should be lubricated sparingly with light grease. Both pallets should be lubricated with either heavy clock oil or light grease. Finally, check that all parts that are supposed to move are free to do so, without binding.

At this stage, the movement is ready for attaching to the seat board. The free end of the lines are threaded through the weight pulleys and then knotted in the seat board. The date wheel pipe and post are cleaned and lubricated before being assembled. The false plate is pinned to the back of the dial and the jumper sparingly lubricated with grease. The last job is fitting the dial and hands to the movement.

The fully assembled movement is placed on a clock horse (test stand) and the pendulum and weights are attached. The movement is wound and test-run for at least a week before fitting it in the case. The clock horse allows unobstructed access to the movement from all sides, making it possible to observe closely the action of the escapement and striking mechanism. A paper or card hood is provided for the movement during the period of testing to offer protection from dust.

The finished clock.

9 SETTING UP THE CLOCK

With all the restoration work completed, the time has come to put the clock in the position it is going to occupy in your home and set it up so that it works properly. Here there are five main criteria to consider: siting the clock; whether or not to fix the clock to the wall; fitting the movement in the case, including pendulum and weights; setting the clock in beat; and finally, regulating the clock.

SITING THE CLOCK

It is very important that the clock is sited in a position that, apart from showing it off to best effect, is conducive to the clock giving its best possible performance, once set up. Any form of cushioned floor covering, particularly a carpet with underlay, is likely to prevent the clock from standing firmly. If the clock does not stand firm it is likely to be troublesome.

Suspended wooden floors in modern family houses are another source of trouble as they are usually far from solid. Although the clock itself may stand firmly on the floor, as soon as somebody walks past it, the floor will flex and the clock will move. In older properties, particularly large houses, suspended floor timbers are usually far more substantial and, as a general rule, present fewer problems. Ideally, the clock should stand directly on a solid quarry tile or parquet floor. If this is not possible, serious consideration should be given to securing the clock to the wall.

Another siting consideration is the proximity of windows, particularly with regard to the effects of sunlight. It would be a pity, having restored your clock, to stand it in direct sunlight and let the case become spoiled and bleached. Also, do not forget that temperature fluctuations will affect the timekeeping qualities of your clock. If you spend a lot of time away from your home you should also consider the security aspect of siting your clock – it is obviously preferable for it not to be easily seen through a window or letter box.

The Importance of Rigidity

Even if your carpet is directly laid on to a solid concrete floor it will still be far from ideal. A thin carpet, with no foam or felt underlay, will still have a certain amount of give in it. All longcase clocks are very top heavy, especially when fully wound. There is the combined weight of the movement and dial plus the pendulum and driving weights, all at the top of the clock. The clock feet are small in area, and closely spaced. With so much weight, right at the top of the case, unless the feet are supported on an absolutely solid surface the clock will not be firm. If the case is allowed to rock, just a little, while the clock is working, this can have an adverse affect on its timekeeping qualities. In severe cases it could easily cause the clock to stop.

You might think that, once wound and set, if nobody goes near the clock there will be nothing to cause it to move and you will have no problems with it. Unfortunately, this is not so. All pendulum clocks have their own built-in medium for causing the clock case to rock on its feet – the pendulum itself, as it swings to and fro. The heavier the pendulum bob, and the larger its swing, the greater this effect will be.

FIXING THE CLOCK TO THE WALL

Even if your clock is standing on a solid floor and is quite firm, it might still be a good idea to secure it to the wall. Longcase clocks do get stolen and anything you can do to deter a thief is worth considering. There is no guarantee that fixing it to the wall will prevent the theft of your clock, but the chances are that it will be ignored for easier pickings.

If you have to stand your clock on a springy floor, or on carpet, then you will have little choice but to secure it to the wall. If the clock is an antique there will, almost certainly, be a number of existing holes through the backboard that were used to fix it to the wall in the past. The best place to secure the clock is as close to the top of the waist section as possible. If the clock is to go flat

Existing array of holes in the backboard.

against the wall it is an easy job to secure it. You will need a piece of batten, the same thickness as the skirting board, and a bit shorter in length than the width of the trunk of the clock. If the batten is too long, it will be easily seen from the side of the clock and look unsightly.

Mark the position on the wall where the batten should be secured, so that it lines up with the holes in the case. When drilling the wall for your fixings, be very careful not to drill through any hidden water pipes or electrical cables. There are special detecting devices available quite cheaply from DIY outlets for scanning walls to find hidden cables and pipes. One screw, with countersunk head, through each end of the batten should be quite sufficient to hold it firmly on the wall.

In the unlikely event that there are no existing holes in your clock case you will have to drill your own. If the clock stands reasonably firmly on the floor, one screw through the case, into the batten will suffice. If, on the other hand, the clock wobbles about easily it would be better to use two screws. Round-head screws should be used to secure the clock to the batten, with a large diameter washer under the screw head to prevent it from biting into the case back when tightened.

It is important that the clock is upright, as far as possible. If it leans back too far the pendulum bob is likely to foul the case back. If it leans forward too far the weights, when they descend, may catch on the step at the bottom of the trunk door. If it leans to one side or the other too far the pendulum bob may foul the case sides. The latter condition rarely occurs as there is usually a fairly generous clearance here unless the angle of the clock case is obvious to the naked eye.

A spirit level will be found useful when fixing your clock to the wall. It may be necessary to use packing between either the skirting board, or the fixing batten, to bring the clock upright when viewed from the side. It is usually sufficient to go by eye when setting it upright when viewed from the front, but a spirit level could be used if preferred.

If the floor is solid but uneven, use thin pieces of wood or plastic placed under the feet of the clock to bring it level and make it stand firmly. Thin pieces of card can be used if it is only slightly out. Even if the clock is going to be secured to the wall, it is still best to level it and ensure that all the feet are supporting their fair share of the weight before fixing it in place. Doing this will help to prevent stressing the case, which might happen if the weight is only supported properly by two or three of the feet.

If you would prefer not to fix your clock to the wall, but are uncertain as to whether or not it is standing firmly enough on the floor, there is a simple test that can be performed to establish this. Take a piece of stiff card (a postcard is perfect for the job), and fold it in half lengthways to make it into a 'V' shape. Place the folded card

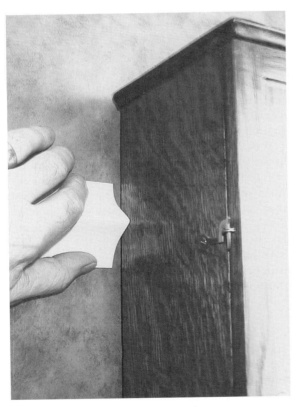

Folded white card held close to the hood, testing for rigidity.

horizontally against the wall, close to the top of the clock. Hold the two edges of the card in firm contact with the wall; Blu-tack can be used here if you prefer, with the crest of the 'V' standing away from the wall. Bring one end of the card up to leave a slight gap at the side of the clock hood. Careful observation of the gap between hood and card, whilst the clock is working, will reveal if it is swaying from side to side.

FITTING THE MOVEMENT TO THE CASE

Remove the hood from the case and open the trunk door. The movement and dial assembly is then lifted on so that the seat board rests on the top of the side cheeks of the case. The lines and pulleys are dropped down inside the trunk of the case. If yours is a thirty-hour movement, with the seat board fixed to the case, then place the movement on top of the seat board and feed the rope or chain down through the central slot.

Before letting go of the movement make absolutely certain it is sitting quite securely. Sometimes a seat board will be distorted, or the side cheeks may have been cut about and are no longer level. At best, under these circumstances, the movement will rock and at worst it may fall and become damaged or cause personal injury. If in doubt, ask someone to steady it for you whilst you find some packing to make it firm.

Before attaching the weights or the pendulum, replace the hood and check to see that the dial is in the centre of the hood aperture, from left to right and top to bottom. If it is not central, then adjust the seat board or use packing until it is. Two more alignments to check are: first that the dial is upright, when viewed from the side, and second that the front to back position is correct. If it is not upright this must be put right with packing. The front to back position should be adjusted so that there is a minimal gap between the dial and the dial aperture in the hood.

When you are satisfied that the dial is properly positioned, remove the hood and attach the pendulum. Check that the pendulum bob is not fouling the backboard; if it is, it will be necessary to take the movement off again and increase the thickness of packing between the top of the clock and the wall. The extra thickness of packing required should be sufficient to ensure that there is at least a minimal clearance between the pendulum bob and the case back.

Next, check that the end of the crutch is not fouling the backboard. If it is touching, the crutch rod should be carefully bent to reduce the clearance between the crutch and the movement back plate. This will automatically increase the clearance at the backboard. It is essential, however, that some clearance is maintained between the crutch and the movement back plate. It is also important to check, after any manipulation of the crutch rod, that the crutch remains perpendicular to the movement back plate. However well the clock has been restored, it will definitely not work properly if either the crutch or the pendulum bob foul anywhere.

The weights are hung last. As already discussed in Chapter One, if the weights are different sizes, the heaviest one usually drives the strike train. You will find it is much easier to hang the weights if the lines are fully unwound. Make certain, before releasing the weight, that the line is properly

around the pulley. Care must be taken, otherwise the line can easily slip off the rim of the pulley just as the weight begins to tension the line. If this is allowed to happen, the line will become wedged between the side of the pulley and its stirrup.

As you wind the clock for the first time, wind slowly, checking after each turn of the key that the line is winding on to the barrel evenly. Once the first few winds are on properly, and the weight is clear of the bottom of the clock, there should be no further cause for concern. If those first few turns of line should be incorrectly spaced on the barrel, they will have to be teased into place with a piece of peg wood or a plastic knitting needle. You will find it easier to do this if the load on the line, where it wraps around the barrel, is eased slightly. To do this, put your hand in through the trunk doorway and grasp the line and gently ease it upwards.

On no account use metal objects to tease the line into place, as this would run the risk of scratching the barrel. The lines may also be abraded and, therefore, weakened. Whenever any work of this sort is undertaken it is always best to wear cotton or linen gloves. It is almost impossible not to leave fingermarks on a movement when working without gloves.

What to do if the Lines are Wound on the Barrels

If for any reason your clock has to be moved, at some later date, you would find it advantageous to let it completely wind down beforehand. If the going side runs down ahead of the strike side, just move the minute hand forward manually to the hour position and allow the strike to run. Repeat this, if necessary, until the strike train is fully wound down. It is then a simple matter to lift off the weights, followed by the pendulum and then remove the movement. When the time comes to reassemble your clock, simply follow the procedure described in the section on 'Fitting the Movement to the Case'.

If you are unable to wait for your clock to wind down, proceed with caution. Do not lift the weights off until you have taken steps to prevent the line from unfurling as the tension is removed. With the weight lifted off, it is surprising how quickly the line can spring away from the barrel and become tangled. If this is allowed to happen it can be a very tedious job to put things right.

One effective method to prevent the lines from coming off is to wrap the barrels with strips of cling film before removing the weights. This will hold the line tightly in contact with the barrel and when the weights have been rehung the cling film is easily removed. It can be a bit of a fiddle to get the cling film to go around the barrels, but a large pair of tweezers will make the job easier. Another advantage with cling film is that it doesn't leave any sticky residue behind after it is removed, unlike some adhesive tapes.

Another method worth considering is to use a large ball of Blu-tack, or similar material. After working it in your hands to make it supple, squeeze it around the line and into the slot in the seat board, from below. This will prevent the line from running back through the seat board when the weight is lifted off. If care is taken,

**What to do if the Lines are Wound
on the Barrels** *continued*

this method will be found sufficient to do the job, although it is not as foolproof as binding the barrels with cling film. If the clicks on the great wheels are in a convenient position, they can be released with a piece of peg wood whilst supporting the weight with the other hand until all the line is wound off.

Once the clock movement has been placed in position, refrain from hanging the weights if the line has furled up inside the movement, or if it has come off the side of the barrel. In the first instance the line may have become tangled around a pin on one of the wheels, or perhaps one of the teeth. If the weight is hung under these conditions it could cause serious damage to the movement. In the latter instance, the line might become tightly wrapped around the barrel arbor and be very difficult to extricate.

If the worst comes to the worst and you do end up with the line resembling a bird's nest inside the movement, and it cannot be untangled, it will have to be cut in several places and removed that way. Fortunately, it is quite easy to fit a new line without dismantling the movement. The old line is removed as described in Chapter Eight. Fitting a new line to an assembled clock is little different from fitting the line when assembling the movement following restoration. If the line winds on from the back of the barrel, as is usual, the job is made a little more awkward because the barrel is obscured, to some extent, by the great wheel and the movement back plate. However, with a little patience it can be done without too much difficulty.

The barrel can easily be turned to bring the hole in its wall to the outside, making it easier to thread the line through. Then, if necessary, it can be turned a little further to line up the large end hole in the barrel with the great wheel crossings. This will enable the end of the line to be pulled through for a short distance and knotted. The line is then pulled back to draw the knot inside the barrel, where it will be anchored. The old knot can be left inside the barrel, as it can do no harm. If, on your clock, the line winds on from the front of the barrel, the job is made easier by not having to worry about the great wheel getting in the way.

Fitting new clock line, barrel end hole at the back of the barrel.

Fitting new clock line, barrel end hole at the front of the barrel.

SETTING A CLOCK IN BEAT

The following procedure can be used to set any longcase clock in beat, recently restored or otherwise. Beat setting is very important. If a clock is 'in beat' it means that the supplementary arc (the overswing of the pendulum, after locking has taken place) is equal when the pendulum swings both to the left and to the right. With the clock working, this will give the characteristic even ticking sound that most people associate with clocks.

If a clock is 'out of beat', the tick will sound very uneven due to the difference in duration of the supplementary arc as the pendulum swings to

Pendulum Protection During Transit

One component frequently damaged when moving a longcase clock is the pendulum rod, particularly the suspension spring. Suspension springs are quite frail and the pendulum rods are easily bent. Pendulum bobs, for English longcase clocks at least, are always heavy and unless precautions are taken it is the movement of the bob, during braking or cornering, which causes the damage to the pendulum.

By far the safest way to transport a longcase pendulum is to remove the pendulum bob first. Before removing the bob, however, it is important to mark its position on the pendulum rod so as to avoid the need for regulating the clock on reassembly. Very often a line is found scratched across the pendulum flat, marking the position of the top of the bob. If there is no line on your clock's pendulum, from a conservation point of view rather than scratching your own, it would be kinder simply to wrap a piece of masking tape around the rod at the appropriate position.

Remove the rating nut and slip the pendulum bob off the rod. Take care to mark the front of the rod first to show which way round it fits in the bob. Replace the rating nut immediately so that it does not get lost. The pendulum bob can now be wrapped and put with the clock weights. The pendulum rod can be strapped to a length of 2in × 1in (50 × 25mm) timber, taking particular care to protect the suspension spring.

A better method would be to use a length of 2in × 2in (50 × 50mm) timber, a little longer than the overall length of the pendulum rod. Ask a local carpentry workshop to run a double-width saw cut down its length and deep enough to take the width of the pendulum flat. Block off the two ends and provide a cover, which could be either hinged or held in place with screws. When the pendulum rod is placed inside the slot, it can be wedged tightly with pieces of cork cut from wine corks, and with the cover secured, it can come to no harm.

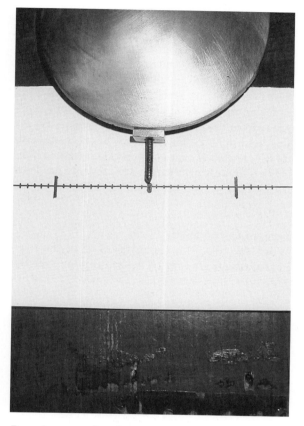

Beat plaque taped to the case back.

and fro. If the supplementary arc reduces to zero on either side, the clock will stop. An outline of the working principles has already been given in Chapter Four, under the heading 'Escapement'.

The best way to check the beat setting is to use a 'beat plaque', which can easily be made from a sheet of white writing paper. To make one, take the piece of paper and cut a rectangle measuring about 6in × 3in (150 × 75mm). Next, draw a line, using a rule lengthways through the centre of the rectangle. Find the approximate centre point of the line and mark it with a dot, just large enough to be clearly seen.

Starting from the centre dot, and working out along the line towards each side of the rectangle, mark off a series of fine cross lines, equally spaced ⅛in (3mm) apart. This will act as the scale of the beat plaque. In theory, the centre line should not be straight at all but drawn at a radius to the point of suspension of the pendulum. However, from a practical point of view it will not matter. Now tape the beat plaque inside the case back, behind the pendulum bob, with the line horizontal and at a height such that the tip of the threaded pendulum rod when at rest is just covering the centre dot.

Carry out the beat test from a kneeling position, directly in front of the pendulum. Slowly move the bob to one side, listening for the clock to tick. At the precise moment that the clock ticks (the 'locking'), mark the position of the end of the pendulum rod on the scale of the beat plaque. Now slowly move the bob the other way and repeat this procedure for the opposite side. These marks are the 'beat points'. The distance between the centre dot, and each beat point, should be equal if the clock is 'in beat'. If the two distances are unequal, the clock is 'out of beat', and an adjustment will have to be made to correct matters.

Adjusting the Beat

When the pendulum is at rest, it is in the mid-beat position (the tip of the pendulum over the centre dot on the beat plaque). With the pendulum in this position, the pendulum rod top block will also hold the crutch in the mid-beat position. It is only the position of the pallets, in relation to the crutch, which needs adjusting to set the clock in beat. The traditional way of making this adjustment is by putting a slight bend in the middle of the crutch rod. The crutch rod should only be bent sufficiently to bring the pallets to the mid-beat position.

As already discussed, always wear cotton gloves before attempting to make any adjustments to the clock movement. Great care should be exercised when bending a crutch rod. If bending is not carried out in the correct manner, damage to the escapement may result. Before an adjustment is made, however, you first have to

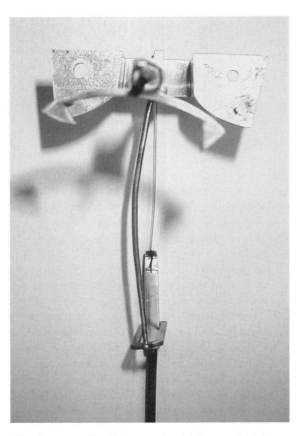

The effect on pallets if the crutch rod is bent to the left.

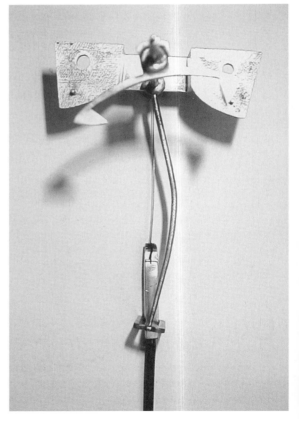

The effect on pallets if the crutch rod is bent to the right.

decide to which side the crutch rod should be bent to bring about the required correction.

The side of the clock having its beat point furthest from the centre dot is the side to which the centre of the crutch rod should be bent to correct the beat. Only a tiny bend is needed; it is easy to go too far. Following adjustment, repeat the beat test again and mark the new beat points on the plaque. The overall distance between the two beat points will always remain the same. After adjustment, one point will have moved closer to the centre dot and the other will have moved further away, by an equal amount. Check to see if they are now equal in distance from the centre dot. You will be very lucky if you get it right with your first adjustment.

The usual way to bend the rod is to stand in front of the clock and bring your hands around to the back of the movement, one from each side. Place the flats of both hands so that they almost touch the movement back plate, keeping your fingers in line. Gently bring your fingertips together, trapping the crutch rod between them. On the side of the crutch rod, represented by the greatest distance between beat point and centre dot, spread your index and second fingers apart so that they bear against, and give support to, the top and bottom of the crutch rod. With the middle finger of the other hand, gently push the centre of the crutch rod from the other side, with just sufficient force to bend the rod slightly. Bending the crutch rod this way restricts all bending stresses to that portion of rod resting between your three fingertips. No other components, or pivots, are stressed in any way. After making adjustments, check that the crutch is still perpendicular to the movement back plate.

One point to bear in mind is that very often antique clocks will suffer from irregularities in the escapement. This could be due to uneven wear on the tips of the escape wheel teeth or perhaps due to the escape wheel going slightly 'out of round' with age. In some cases, if the collet has been moved, the escape wheel may no longer be concentric with its arbor. It is also possible that the escape wheel arbor could be slightly bent, causing the escape wheel to rotate eccentrically. Wear on the pallet locking surfaces or the escape

wheel and pallet arbor pivots and pivot holes will also affect the escapement action.

Because of these irregularities, beat setting can only ever be a compromise, based on the combined effect of all the escapement errors. Therefore, after following the above procedures to bring the clock in beat, unless the escapement errors are very slight, you will have to make fine adjustments by ear. To achieve the best performance from the clock, the beat should be set to a mean average of the errors during one complete revolution of the escape wheel.

Start the clock going by moving the pendulum bob 2½in (64mm) to one side, keeping it parallel with the backboard, and then release it. Allow the clock to run for a few minutes so that the

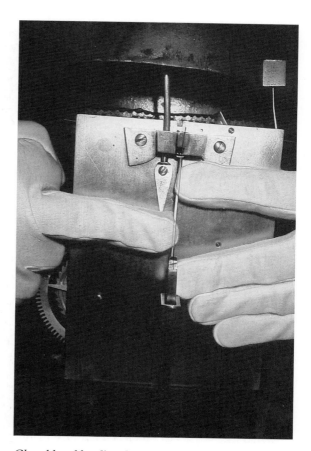

Gloved hand bending the crutch rod, viewed from behind the movement.

pendulum can settle to its natural rhythm. Listen carefully to each beat of the clock, as the escape wheel makes one full revolution. As you listen, observe the tip of the pendulum rod against your beat plaque. The tick will be heard just as the pendulum tip reaches the beat marks. After the tick is heard, the tip of the pendulum will continue to swing a little way past the mark (the supplementary arc).

Providing that the supplementary arc is more or less equal on both sides of the beat plaque, during one full revolution of the escape wheel, the clock is in beat. If, on average, it is found to be greater on one side than the other, you will need to make an adjustment to the crutch rod in order to correct matters.

REGULATING A CLOCK

Regulating a clock is a very easy task to perform. If a well-maintained clock is kept at a fairly constant temperature and humidity throughout the year, it can be expected to keep excellent time, closer than one minute per month. There are no hard and fast rules governing how many turns of the rating nut will be required to bring a clock to time – it depends on a number of variable factors. Fortunately, there is a simple procedure that can be adopted to make the job of regulating any pendulum clock quicker and easier than just relying on trial and error adjustments.

If the clock has recently been moved from one place to another, providing due care has been taken with the pendulum, little regulation should be required. Looking up at the pendulum bob from below, the rating nut is turned clockwise (raising the pendulum bob) to make the clock go faster and anti-clockwise (lowering the bob) to make it go slower. If the timekeeping is only out by a few minutes a week it will suffice to adjust the rating nut by half a turn or so, in the appropriate direction, each time the clock is wound, until it is brought to time.

When the error is much greater, following repairs to a pendulum rod or replacing a broken suspension spring for instance, then a greater degree of regulation may be required to bring the clock to time. If you were to rely on making small adjustments to the rating nut, when winding the clock, regulation could take weeks to complete.

If timekeeping is found to be a long way out, the following procedure can be used to speed up the process of regulation. Set the clock to the exact time and make a note of how many minutes the clock gains, or loses, in a twenty-four-hour period. Mark a spot on the front of the rating nut with paint or marker pen – this will make observation easier, to ensure that the nut is only given full turns.

Turn the rating nut, in the appropriate direction, depending on whether the clock is gaining or losing. The number of turns given to the rating nut should be sufficient to make a noticeable difference to regulation and this number should be noted down. Generally, ten full turns should suffice. However, if the thread for the rating nut is very fine, twenty turns would be better.

Set the clock to the exact time and let it run for another twenty-four hours and then, just as before, make a note of how many minutes the clock has either gained or lost. Now compare the two readings and write down the difference between them. Express the difference as 'minutes per twenty-four hours'. The clock will now be either closer to time or you may have over-compensated. It will not matter which for our purposes.

All you have to do now is divide the number of turns you made to the rating nut by the number of minutes difference in rate it produced, per twenty-four-hour period. This will give you the number of turns, or part turns, required of the rating nut to produce a change in rate of one minute per twenty-four hours. This value should be written on the beat plaque for future reference.

For the first few weeks of running, following restoration or being moved to a new location, it may be necessary to regulate a clock, until it settles down. Once this initial settling-in period is over, the clock should maintain a good rate.

It is a good idea to make a diary note to remind yourself, in five years' time, that the movement will need oiling. It is as well not to run a clock for more than five years between periods of oiling to

Example Rating Calculation

Let us assume the clock has been set up and that the hands were set to the correct time. After running for twenty-four hours, it is found that the clock has lost five and a half minutes (the clock has a losing rate). To make the clock go faster you must raise the pendulum bob and so the rating nut must be turned in a clockwise direction, when viewed from below. Give the rating nut exactly ten full turns (the dot of paint on the rating nut will make this easy) then reset the hands of the clock to the correct time. Allow the clock to run for another twenty-four hours and then check the rate again. Let us assume, this time, that the clock has gained two minutes in twenty-four hours (the clock has a gaining rate).

Calculation
The number of full turns given to the rating nut *divided by* the number of minutes difference in rate for the two rating checks:

- first rate check $= -5.5\text{min}$
- second rate check $= +2\text{min}$
- difference in rate $= 7.5\text{min per 24 hours.}$

Therefore:

10 divided by 7.5 $= 1.33$
1.33 turns of the rating nut $= 1\text{min in 24 hours change in rate.}$

We know, after the last adjustment, that the clock now has a gaining rate of two minutes in twenty-four hours, and we now know that 1.33 turns of the rating nut will change the rate of the clock by one minute in twenty-four hours.

Therefore:

$2 \times 1.33 = 2.66$ or two and two-thirds of a turn on the rating nut, anti-clockwise to slow it down, will bring the clock to time.

The accuracy of this method does rely on the following points:

1. All rating checks must be compared with a time source of known accuracy.
2. The time period used for conducting rating checks must be exactly twenty-four hours.
3. During the test, the rating nut must only be given complete turns.
4. The clock hands must be set to the correct time at the commencement of each rating check.

avoid the risk of it running dry. It will also give you the opportunity to check the movement thoroughly for early signs of pending trouble. Prevention is always better than cure.

To oil a clock movement properly it must be removed from the clock case and it is necessary to remove both the hands and the dial. We have already discussed the importance of putting just the right amount of oil in the exact spot that it is needed. It is virtually impossible to do this properly with the dial in place.

The case will benefit from the application of a good quality wax polish, at the least every three months. If the clock's environment is hot and dry, more frequent polishing would be beneficial. Dust should be removed from the dial of a clock with a soft brush, taking care not to damage the hands.

If you follow these simple guidelines you can expect your longcase clock to give you a lifetime's service. Not only this, but you will have a treasured family heirloom that you can hand down to future generations in your family.

10 MAKING YOUR OWN CLOCK CASE

There are three different routes you can choose if you would like to build your own clock case. The easiest and quickest way is to buy a complete longcase clock kit, which would include everything necessary to build a complete clock. Another way is to buy the plans for the style of clock case that appeals to you, and have it made by a cabinetmaker, in the wood of your choice. Finally, if you have the skills and the facilities, you could make the case yourself from a set of plans, or even design your own.

MAKING A CLOCK FROM A KIT

There are suppliers of clock materials (*see* Further Information) who offer a choice of longcase clock kits. There are some excellent kits available, made from a choice of solid hardwoods and, with a little work, a good quality clock can be produced from these. Usually, all clock kits are supplied complete, with all necessary fittings, screws and a full set of instructions. The only items not normally supplied are adhesives, stains, polishes and glass. You will need to source these yourself from your local DIY store.

Although building from a kit is, without doubt, the easiest, quickest and most economical way of building your own clock, there is a downside of which you should be aware. Some of the kits offered are designed and produced to satisfy the less discerning budget market. Case styles are usually limited to the very basic, and the materials used tend to be veneered plywood or MDF. Few of the joints will be traditionally made, the preference being for adhesive-free, quick assembly fasteners.

One problem encountered with most kits is the fact that, in the interest of simplicity and

cost, the hoods are integral with the case and, therefore, non-detachable. This makes it difficult to get at the movement if adjustments become necessary, including setting the clock in beat. If adjustments are required, it may be necessary to move the clock away from the wall to access the movement from behind. However, it is sometimes possible to make a beat adjustment by putting your hand up to the movement through the trunk door of the clock.

Beat Setting on Modern Movements

Beat setting on modern movements does not involve bending the crutch rod, as discussed for antique movements. The crutch rod is attached to the pallet arbor using a special collet, which gives a fairly tight friction fit between these two components. The friction collet enables the crutch rod to be manually turned on the pallet arbor, allowing the angular disposition between them to be changed. Many modern movements will automatically self set in beat if the pendulum is given a good swing.

If a beat plaque is used, as outlined in Chapter Nine, this will indicate which way the crutch should be moved to put the clock in beat. Then, instead of trying to bend the crutch rod, simply lift off the pendulum and gently move the crutch to whichever side it needs to go, using the tip of your finger. Keep moving it until a resistance is felt; then, give a very slight extra push with your fingertip, against the resistance. This will move the crutch rod on the pallet arbor and change the beat setting.

It should be pointed out that when adjusting the beat on a modern movement in this way, the crutch should be moved to the side, opposite that indicated in Chapter Nine. Consider for a

Yet another variation is a crutch rod made up of two halves riveted together in the middle, with a large single rivet, forming a friction joint. This allows beat setting by angling the joint slightly, either to the left or to the right. A moment's thought will show that this latter idea will produce exactly the same effect as bending the crutch rod on an antique clock, as described in Chapter Nine.

Unlike antique clocks, the pendulums of modern movements do not have a suspension spring attached to their ends. Modern suspension springs are very short and the top of the spring is pinned to the back cock to prevent it from coming off. It is also rare for the pendulum to attach directly on to the other end of the suspension spring. Usually there is a device called a 'pendulum leader', made from a narrow strip of brass about 4in (100mm) long, and this hooks on to the bottom of the suspension spring. The pendulum hooks on to the bottom of the pendulum leader, and the crutch, in this case, connects with the lower half of the pendulum leader.

It is important to emphasize that when adjusting the beat setting the pendulum should first be unhooked from the pendulum leader. Also, to make the adjustment, the tip of your finger must bear against the side of the crutch, not the pendulum leader. If the pendulum leader is pushed it is likely to flex just a little and then spring back again. If too much pressure is applied to the pendulum leader it could damage the suspension spring.

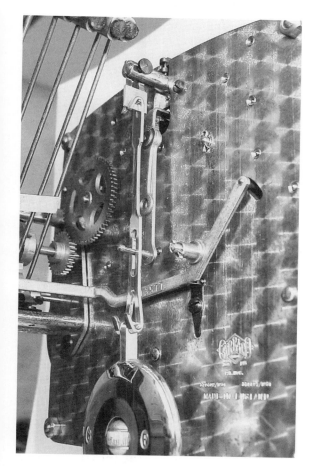

A modern suspension spring, pendulum leader and pendulum assembly.

moment supporting an antique crutch rod at the top and bottom and then bending the middle to one side, as described in Chapter Nine. The effect on the pallets will be the same as bending the bottom of the rod the opposite way.

Occasionally, on some modern movements, beat adjustment is effected by means of a large knurled screw, situated near one end of the crutch rod. If the screw is situated right at the top of the rod, turning it changes the angular disposition between the crutch rod and the pallet arbor. If the screw is situated at the bottom of the crutch rod, turning it just offsets the position of the crutch in relation to the crutch rod. Both are equally effective in providing beat adjustment.

MAKING A CLOCK FROM PLANS

Longcase clock plans, for various case styles, are advertised for sale by a number of clock material suppliers (*see* Further Information). Usually (although it is worth checking before buying), plans come complete with a full cutting list and a schedule of operations. These details help when costing the materials and labour, and reduce the risk of errors during subsequent manufacture.

The big advantage with making your own clock is that you can select the exact style of clock case that appeals to you the most. You can also decide which type of wood you would like it to be made from, the finish given to it, and the type of dial and movement used. If professionally drawn-up plans are used to make the case it is very likely that the finished article will closely resemble a genuine antique case of similar style, in both quality and appearance.

If you do not have the necessary facilities and skills to make the case yourself, you could ask a local cabinetmaker to quote for making the

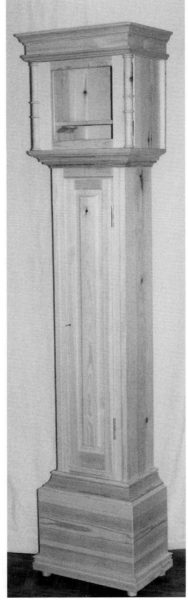

Pine case without hood.

Pine case with hood fitted.

The finished clock.

case to your plans, and in the wood of your choice. An elaborate case style, in an exotic wood, is likely to be very costly, but a fairly plain style in oak will cost a lot less. If a country-style case, made in pine, appeals to you, any competent joiner could make a very acceptable case at quite modest cost.

The first clock case, illustrated here, was made by a joiner, from a set of commercially available plans described as 'seventeenth-century longcase clock'. The case was made in pine and given a dark antique finish. The construction details were fairly closely followed, although the joiner was given leave to vary things to suit the materials he had available and to simplify some aspects of the design. The total cost of the bare case (without its finish or glass) delivered to the door was £455. There was no VAT as the joiner was not VAT-registered.

There are many different wood finishes available today, particularly for pine, which is a popular wood. Some of the finishes are oil- or spirit-based, but increasingly water-based products are being manufactured and these are very easy to apply with a brush. Once you have your case, the final choice, regarding finish, is yours.

This clock case was designed to take a modern German chiming movement and square dial. The material dealers offer a range of movements and dials to suit. The movement selected offers a choice of three different chimes and incorporates automatic night silencing of both strike and chimes. The strike and chimes are struck on a twelve-rod gong that was supplied with the movement. The pendulum rod is wood and the pendulum bob and weight shells are satin-finished brass. The total cost of the movement and dial, including gong, weights and pendulum, was £320 including delivery and VAT. The finishing materials and glass cost £30, giving a total cost for this clock of £775.

The second clock illustrated was made from a kit manufactured by the 'Emperor Clock Company' in the USA (*see* Further Information) but purchased from its UK supplier. The company manufactures several different models, although not all are imported into the UK.

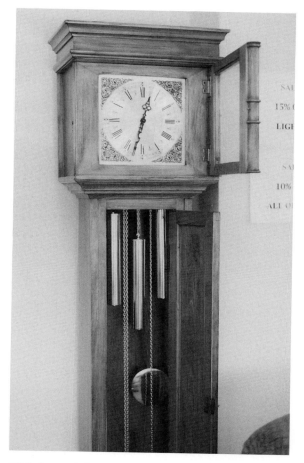

With the trunk door open to show the weights and pendulum.

They are available either as kits or fully assembled cases. The model illustrated is made from solid cherry wood, except for the backboard which is made in plywood. Oak and American black walnut are also available. The cost of this particular kit, in round figures, was £800 in 2001, but has since been discontinued.

As with the first clock, the assembly instructions were not followed exactly, a few slight changes being made to accommodate personal choice. Proper locks were fitted in place of the magnetic catches supplied, and the brass-plated steel hinges were replaced in favour of solid brass. The gong mounting was modified to enable the larger, and more expensive, triple chime movement to be used. Also, bevel-edged glass was fitted to both the hood and trunk doors, instead of flat glass, improving the appearance of the clock. The glass and other extra costs for this clock came to £100, giving a total cost of £900 for the complete clock (2001 prices).

The triple chime movement is exactly the same as that used in the first clock illustrated, but this time the dial is a break arch with moon phase indication. Also, because there is a glazed trunk door, a more attractive lyre pendulum has been used and the weight shells and pendulum bob are polished brass. If a traditional longcase movement is required, striking the hours only on a bell, new ones are available from J.M.W. Clocks (*see* Further Information). These move-

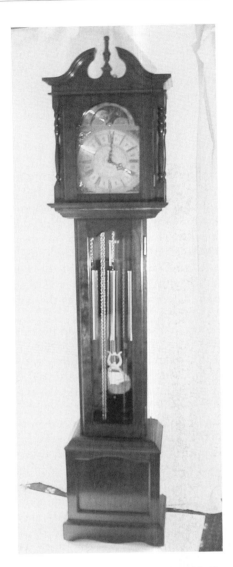

A good-quality, hardwood clock case built from a kit.

The movement fitted to the clock.

ments are of traditional design, except for the pendulum, which screws together in sections for convenience of carriage. Movements are supplied fully assembled and finished; either way, they come complete with square dial and serpentine-style hands as standard. Other dial types can be supplied and would be quoted at extra cost. The cost of the movement is around £850 including delivery.

Dial with the hood door open.

Classic longcase movement supplied by Devon Clocks.

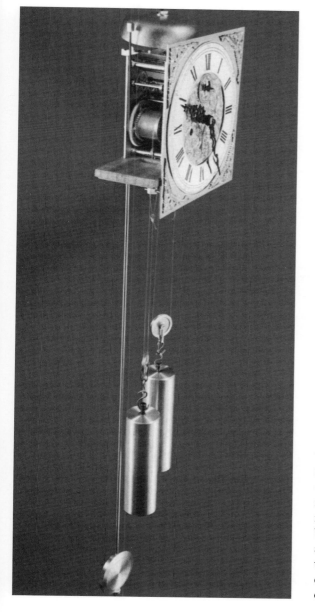

Buying a Ready-Made Case

If, after comparing costs and specifications, you decide to buy a ready-made case from a supplier, establish the make and model of both the movement and dial that the case has been designed to accept. It would also be advisable before purchasing the case to check that both are still readily available. If an alternative movement and dial have to be used, modifications may be required before achieving a good fit.

Although clock kits would come complete with a movement and dial, when making a case from a set of plans it is advisable to choose and purchase the movement and dial you intend to use prior to making the case. This will allow you to assemble the dial and movement and double-check the measurements to ensure a proper fit when the case is completed. You might find it necessary to make slight alterations to the size of the dial surround in the hood, or to vary the height of the seat board to accommodate your choice of movement and dial. If you leave this measurement check until after the case has been made, and you then discover a problem, it will cause you a great deal of consternation and time-wasting.

FURTHER INFORMATION

BIBLIOGRAPHY

Baillie, G H, *Watchmakers and Clockmakers of the World*, Volume 1 (NAG Press, 1996), ISBN 0 7198 0040 4

Conservation of Clocks and Watches (The British Horological Institute Ltd, 1995), ISBN 0 9509621 4 7

DeCarle, Donald, *Practical Clock Repairing*, 3rd edition (NAG Press, 1969), ISBN 0 7198 0000 5

Loomes, Brian, *Grandfather Clocks and Their Cases* (Bracken Books, 1985), ISBN 1 85170 3764

Loomes, Brian, *Watchmakers and Clockmakers of the World*, Volume 2 (NAG Press, 1989) ISBN 0 7198 0250 4

Miller's Clocks and Barometers Buyer's Guide (Reed International Books, 1997), ISBN 1 85732 990 2

Tennant, M F, *Long Case Painted Dials: Their History and Restoration* (NAG Press, 1995), ISBN 0 7198 0260 1

MAGAZINES

Clocks Magazine
Splat Publishing Ltd, 28 Gillespie Crescent, Edinburgh EH10 4HU, Scotland
Tel: 0131 331 3200; Fax: 0131 331 3213
www.clocksmagazine.com

Horological Journal
The British Horological Institute, Upton Hall, Newark, Nottinghamshire NG23 5TE, England
Tel: 01636 813795
www.bhi.co.uk

HOROLOGICAL ORGANIZATIONS

The British Horological Institute Limited
Upton Hall, Upton, Newark, Nottinghamshire NG23 5TE, England
Tel: 01636 813795; Fax: 01636 812258
www.bhi.co.uk

Antiquarian Horological Society
New House, High Street, Ticehurst, Wadhurst, East Sussex TN5 7AL, England
Tel: 01580 200155; Fax: 01580 201323
www.ahsoc.co.uk

American Watchmakers/Clockmakers Institute
701 Enterprise Drive, Harrison, OH, 45030–1697, USA
www.awci.com

National Association of Watch and Clock Collectors Inc.
514 Poplar Street, Columbia, PA, 17512, USA
www.nawcc.org

Horological Guild of Australasia
PO Box 2104, Mt Waverley, Victoria 3149

Jewelers and Watchmakers of New Zealand
www.jwnz.co.nz

SUPPLIERS OF CLOCK KITS, PLANS, FINISHED CASES, MOVEMENTS AND ANCILLARIES

Martin H Dunn
Glebe Farm, Clarks Road, North Killingholme,

North Lincolnshire DN40 3JQ, England
Tel: 01469 540901; Fax: 01469 541512
www.clocksnbits.co.uk

H S Walsh & Sons Ltd
243 Beckenham Road, Beckenham, Kent BR3
4TS, England
Tel: 0208 778 7061; Fax: 0208 676 8669
www.hswalsh.com

J M W Clocks
12 Norton Green Close, Sheffield S8 8BP,
England
Tel: 0114 2745693; Fax: 0114 2740295
www.j-m-w.co.uk

Timecraft
Unit 19, Sefton Lane, Sefton Lane Industrial
Estate, Maghull, Liverpool L31 8BX, England
Tel: 0151 526 2516; Fax: 0151 526 4455
www.timecraft.co.uk

Emperor Clock Company
www.emperorclocks.com

Craft Supplies Ltd
www.craft-supplies.com

Oakside Classic Clocks
Tel: 0118 9701 377
www.classic-clocks.co.uk

Mills & Sons
15 Townsend Lane, Long Lawford, Rugby,
Warwickshire CV23 9DQ, England
Tel: 01788 565268
www.millsandsons.co.uk

Olivers
15 Cross Street, Hove, Sussex BN3 1AJ,
England
Tel: 01273 736542
(Old clocks for restoration, movements, dials,
parts, etc.)

G K Hadfield
Old Post Office, Great Salkeld, Penrith,
Cumbria CA11 9LW, England
Tel/Fax: 01768 870111
www.gkhadfield-tilly.co.uk

HOROLOGICAL EDUCATION AND TRAINING ORGANIZATIONS

The British Horological Institute Ltd
(Listed opposite)

**National Association of Watch and Clock
Collectors Inc**.
(Listed opposite)

West Dean College
West Dean, Chichester, West Sussex PO18
0QZ, England
Tel: 01243 818299
www.westdean.org.uk

USEFUL CONTACTS

Antique Horology www.antique-horology.org;
up-to-date lists of antique fairs and auctions.

Horological Fairs
(Regular horological fairs held in London and
Birmingham)
www.clocksandwatchfairs.com

Penman Fairs
(Antique fairs held at Chelsea, Kensington,
Chester and Sussex)
www.penman-fairs.co.uk

HOROLOGICAL BOOK SUPPLIERS

G K Hadfield
Old Post Office, Great Salkeld, Penrith,
Cumbria CA11 9LW, England
Tel/Fax: 01768 870111
www.gkhadfield-tilly.co.uk

Shenton Books
La Rochelle, Venns Gate, Cheddar, Somerset
BS27 3BY, England
Tel: 0845 838 5523
www.shentonbooks.com

US Books
www.usbooks.com

Arlington Book Company Inc
www.arlingtonbooks.com

GLOSSARY

Amplitude The amount of swing of the pendulum, its arc of vibration.

Anchor Escapement Another name given to the 'recoil' escapement.

Arbor The shaft or axle carrying wheels and pinions that turns in bearings between the clock plates.

Arkansas Stone A fine abrasive stone, hard and white in colour, leaves a smooth surface.

BA (British Association) A system of screw threads used in English clocks and instruments, etc.

Beat The tick as one tooth of the escape wheel drops on to the locking face of a pallet.

Beat (in) The even ticking sound achieved when the supplementary arc is equal for each beat of the pendulum.

Beat (out) The uneven or lame ticking sound heard when the escapement is maladjusted. The supplementary arcs, as the pendulum swings to the left and right, being of unequal duration.

Bluing The process of colouring polished steel to a deep blue by heating it to 300°C (570°F).

Bob The weight (usually lenticular in shape) at the lower end of the pendulum rod.

Break Arch An arch at the top of a dial or hood, set in at both sides leaving a shoulder or step, creating a 'broken arch'.

Bridge A supporting bracket or bearing plate secured in position by two mounting feet.

Broach A long tapered tool, five sided for cutting or round for burnishing. Used to finish holes.

Buff Stick A flat stick with a strip of abrasive paper glued to it, available in various grades. Used for finishing metal surfaces.

Burnisher A piece of hard steel, of suitable section, dressed with a fine cross grain using an oil stone. Used to polish metal by rubbing it across the surface to be finished.

Carborundum Stone A fast-cutting abrasive block available in grades from fine to coarse.

Cartouche A small decorative plaque, usually in the form of a tablet or shield.

Chapter Ring The ring bearing the numbers one to twelve and the minutes, on a clock dial.

Click The mechanism which allows a ratchet wheel to turn independently, in one direction only.

Cock A supporting bracket or bearing plate secured in position by only one mounting foot.

Collet A boss sometimes used for mounting wheels to arbors. A disc of material used to assist in holding a clock hand in position. A lathe attachment used for accurate work holding, sometimes referred to as split chucks or wire chucks.

Compensating Pendulum A pendulum employing some means of automatically compensating for changes in length caused by temperature variations.

Crossings The arms or spokes of wheels.

Crutch The mechanism which connects the escapement to the pendulum.

Depth The degree of meshing between a wheel and pinion.

Detent A form of stop or locking mechanism.

Dial Feet The pillars attached to the back of a dial by which the dial is accurately positioned on the movement front plate or false plate.

Drop The action of an escape wheel tooth 'dropping' on to a pallet locking face, following the release of a tooth by the other pallet. The drop should be equal on both pallets.

End Shake The axial or in-line clearance of an arbor between the clock plates.

Entry Pallet The first pallet reached by an advancing escape wheel tooth.

Escapement The mechanism responsible for allowing the going train to advance by a measured amount at each beat of the pendulum.

Exit Pallet The second pallet reached by an advancing escape wheel tooth.

False Plate A plate sometimes found fitted between the dial and movement front plate.

Fly The speed regulator or governor for the strike train.

Gathering Pallet A device for gathering up the rack, one tooth at a time, also provided with a long tail for locking the strike train after gathering the last tooth on the rack.

Head Stock The main component of a lathe containing the drive spindle and pulley.

Horology The art and science of mechanical time measurement and indication.

Horologist One who practises horology.

Impulse The small energy input delivered by the escapement to the pendulum at each beat.

Jacot Tool Supplied as a lathe attachment for the use of repairing and burnishing pivots.

Lenticular Shaped like a lens of biconvex form.

Oil Sink The spherical depression around the pivot holes, designed to hold a small reserve of oil.

Pallets The component that controls the escape wheel, allowing it to turn a measured amount at each beat of the pendulum, simultaneously imparting a small restoring impulse to the pendulum.

Peg Wood Short sticks of wood available in different diameters, the ends are sharpened and used to clean or 'peg out' pivot holes.

Pinion Small toothed cog wheel, usually made integral with the steel arbor.

Pivot The horological name for the bearings at the end of arbors.

Pivot Hole The bearing holes in which pivots run.

Potence or **Potance** The name used to describe a 'cock' when it is fitted between the clock plates as opposed to the outside surfaces.

Rack One of the main components used to control the number of hammer blows struck on the bell of some striking clocks.

Recoil The slight reversal of rotation made by the escape wheel during the supplementary arc of the pendulum.

Shake Working clearance, particularly between pivots and pivot holes.

Side Shake The side clearance between a pivot and pivot hole.

Soft Jaws Lining for vice jaws to protect delicate surfaces from damage whilst being gripped. Sometimes called 'chops' or 'clams'.

Spandrels The triangular gilded brass castings mounted in the four corners of early clock dials. On later painted dials there would usually be a painted decoration or perhaps a pastoral scene instead.

Spindle Usually refers to the main hollow driving shaft of the lathe.

Supplementary Arc The continued arc of vibration, or over-swing, of the pendulum which takes place after a tooth of the escape wheel has dropped and locked on a pallet locking face.

Train The name given to a set of wheels and pinions forming a gear train in a clock. Usually there is a 'strike train' and a 'going train'.

INDEX

anchor escapement 30
Arabic numerals 91
auctions 15–16, 17–18
    problems 23–4

back cock 30, 35–6
barrel 27, 28
beat plaque 127, 132
beat setting, antique movements
    126–30
    adjusting 128–30
    testing 127–8
beat setting, modern
    movements 132–3
bell 44
bill of sale 22
birdcage movement 11
bluing 94
break-arch dial 6, 7
bushing 110–12
buying a clock 15–24
    from antique shops 17
    from auctions 15–16, 17–18,
      23–4
    from classified ads 17, 24
    from dealers 16
    from fairs 18
    on-line 18
    pitfalls 20–4
    receipts 22

cannon pinion 38–41, 42
    thirty-hour 55
case furniture 5
case making 132–7
    from a kit 132–3
case materials 5–6
case rebuilds 21
case restoration
    assessing 63–6

dismantling 76
drying and shrinkage damage
    62–3
finishing 85–6
reassembly 82–5
repair 76–81
case types 6
cases, mass-produced 5–6
chalk brushing 117
chiming movements 12–13
cleaning a movement 117–18
click and ratchet wheel 28, 30
collet 30
conservation versus restoration
    22–3, 74
count wheel strike 43, 53–61
    eight-day 59
    hour counting mechanism
      54–5
    how it works 55–7
    problems 59–61
    strike release and run to
      warning mechanism 55
    strike train 53
    variations 58
crutch 31
crutch rod 30–1

date wheels 88
dial and movement marriages
    20–1
dial restoration 86–93
dial signatures 91
dial types 6–9
    break-arch 69
    drum head 6
    oval 67
    painted 7
    regulator 9
    round 6, 7

square 7
dials, restoration of 22, 67–8,
    72–3
driving weights 13–14
drum head clocks 6

eight-day clocks count wheel
    strike 59
escape wheel 29–34
escapement 25, 30–4
    function of 31
    motion work 37–42
    oscillator 34–7
    power source 26–7
    rack strike 43–52
    value 15
    wheel train 28–30

floor, suitable, for clock 122
fly 43

gathering pallet 46, 48, 49, 50,
    52
glue, deterioration of 63
granddaughter clock 6
grandfather clock 6
'Grandfather's Clock' (song) 6,
    14
grandmother clock 6

hammer arm 44
hammer lifting tail 45–6
hammer tail 45
hand collet 38–40, 96
hands 8, 9
    assessing for restoration
      67–8
    hour hand 42
    minute hand 38–41
    restoration 94–6

Harrison, John 37
hoop wheel 53, 56, 57
hoop wheel detent 53, 54
hour bridge pipe 42
hour-counting mechanism,
    count wheel strike 54–5
hour-counting mechanism, rack
    strike 46–9
hour hand 42
hour pipe 42
hour snail 46, 48–9, 50, 51
hour wheel 37, 41–2, 49

idler pulley 26–7
incomplete clocks, sale of 21–2

Jacot drum 106–8
jumper 88

key plate 28, 29
kits, longcase making 132,
    135–7

leaf spring 45
lenticular glass 6
lifting piece 49, 50, 61
lines 27, 125–6
locking 32–3
locking detent arbor 53
locking lifting arm 55

*Miller's Clocks and Barometers
    Buyer's Guide* 16
minute hand 38–41
minute pinion 41
minute spring 38–40
minute wheel 38–41, 42, 50
modern movements, beat
    adjustment on 132–3
moon phase feature 7
motion work 25, 37–42
movement, fitting to case
    124–6
movement, five subsections of
    25
movement, restoration 73,
    97–121
    assembly 118–21
    cleaning 117–18

dismantling 99–105
repairing 105–16
trial assembly 116
movements, antique 9–12
movements, chiming 10, 12–13
movements, reproduction 13

numerals, styles of 91

oiling 69, 119–20, 131
oscillator 25, 34–7

pallets 30–4
pendulum 6, 34–7
    attaching 124–5
    leader 133
    length 36–7
    temperature compensated
        37
    transporting 127
pendulum bob 36
pendulum flat 36
pendulum rod 35–6
pin wheel 43, 44, 45, 52
plans, casemaking from 133–7
posted movement 11
power source 25, 26–7
price guide 15–16
professional qualifications 70

quarter-chiming movements
    12–13

rack 46–7, 49–52
rack hook 46, 47, 49–52
rack spring 46, 47, 50–2
rack tail 47, 50
    sprung 115
rack strike 43–52
    hour counting mechanism
        46–9
    how it works 50–2
    strike release and run-to-
        warning mechanism 49
    strike train 43–5
    thirty-hour 58–9
rating calculation 131
ready-made cases 137
regulating a clock 130–1

regulator clocks 6
    dials 9
reproduction movements 13
restoration, professional 68–73
    of case 74–86
    of dial 86–93
    of hands 94–6
    of movement 97–121
    resumé of costs 120
    time taken 120
restoration work, bad 22–3
rigidity, for siting clock 122,
    124
rocking features 7–9
Roman numerals 91

seat board 26, 27
setting up a clock 122–31
shake 99
siting a clock 122
spandrels 9
strike trains 43–61; *see under*
    count wheel strike; rack
    strike
striking problems 59–61
sunlight, effects of 122
supplementary arc 33
suspension spring 35–6

thirty-hour clocks 11–12
    count wheel strike 43, 53–8
    rack strike 58–9
    value 15
three-train (chiming)
    movements 12–13
time train 25–42
train count 105

under-dial work 46

values of antique clocks 15–16

wall, fixing clock to 123–4
warning piece 49, 50
warning wheel 43, 44, 50, 51
weights 26–7
    hanging 125
wheel train 25, 38
white dials 7